MathFlare

Name: ____________________________

Class: ___________

Teacher: ____________________________

Introduction

As parents and educators, we recognize the pivotal role mathematics plays in shaping a child's academic journey and future success. Yet, the path to mathematical proficiency can often seem daunting, fraught with challenges and complexities. That's where the transformative power of MathFlare Workbooks shine through, illuminating the way forward with clarity, precision, and purpose.

Introducing MathFlare Workbooks – a beacon of guidance, a testament to excellence, and a catalyst for achievement. Crafted with meticulous care and expertise, MathFlare Workbooks stand as paragons of educational excellence, designed to nurture young minds, ignite a passion for learning, and develop a deep-rooted understanding of mathematical concepts.

Picture this: your child eagerly delves into the pages of Mathflare Workbook, greeted by a step-by-step guide illuminated with vivid examples that demystify complex mathematical concepts. With each turn of the page, they embark on a journey of discovery, encountering thoughtfully curated practice questions that reinforce learning and hone problem-solving skills. And when they unveil the answers to those very questions, a sense of accomplishment blossoms within them – a tangible reward for their hard work and dedication.

But MathFlare Workbooks are more than just tools for learning; they are pathways to comprehension, fostering a deep-seated understanding of mathematical concepts through a sequential, logical flow. From fundamental principles to advanced problem-solving strategies, every chapter builds upon the last, ensuring a robust foundation upon which future knowledge can be constructed.

As parents, we yearn for nothing more than to see our children thrive, to witness the spark of inspiration ignited within them as they conquer academic challenges with confidence and poise. MathFlare Workbooks serve as partners in this noble endeavor, offering not just practice questions, but the keys to unlocking a world of opportunity.

And for teachers, MathFlare Workbooks stand as invaluable allies in the quest to cultivate mathematical proficiency in the classroom. With answers readily available, instructors can focus on guiding and nurturing their students, confident in the knowledge that MathFlare Workbooks provide a solid framework upon which to build.

In the pages of MathFlare Workbooks, we find not just the promise of academic excellence, but the seeds of a brighter tomorrow. So let us embrace the power of mathematics, let us champion the journey of learning, and let us pave the way for a generation of young minds poised to shape the world. With MathFlare Workbooks as our guide, the possibilities are infinite, and the future, bright.

Table of Contents

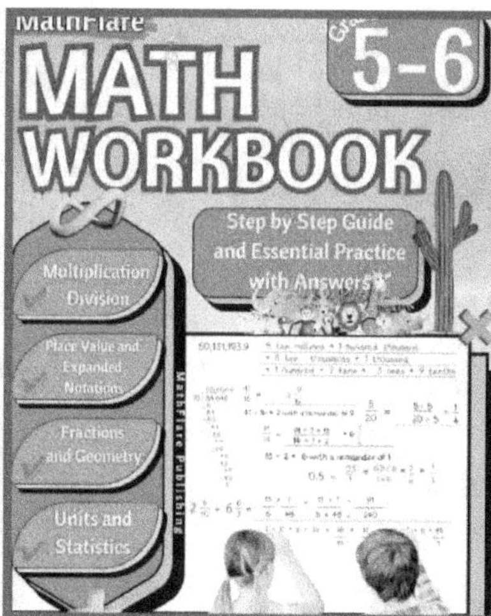

Fractions

Fractions represent parts of a whole. They consist of a numerator (the number on top) and a denominator (the number on the bottom).

For example: we have an orange, and we divide it into 5 equal slices. Each slice represents $\frac{1}{5}$ of the orange. Now, if we take 3 of those slices, we have taken $\frac{3}{5}$ of the orange.

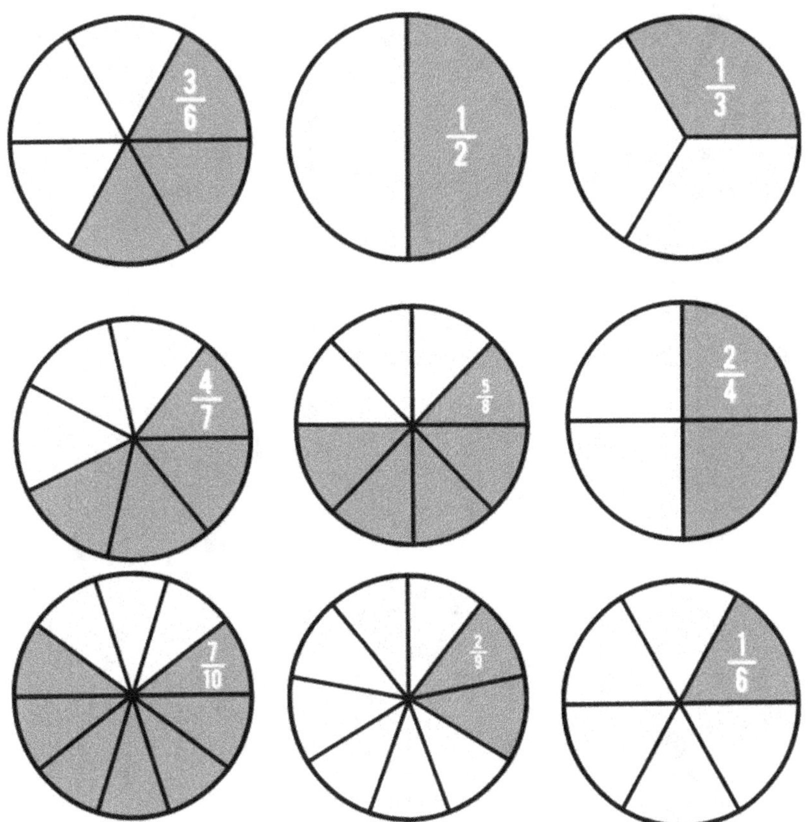

Equivalent Fractions

Equivalent fractions are fractions that represent the same value or part of a whole, even though they may look different.

To find equivalent fractions, you can:

- Multiply or divide both the numerator and denominator by the same nonzero number.
- Simplify fractions to their simplest form.

$\frac{1}{2}$ and $\frac{2}{4}$ are equivalent fractions because if you multiply the numerator and denominator of $\frac{1}{2}$ by 2, you get $\frac{2}{4}$. Similarly, if you divide both the numerator and denominator of $\frac{2}{4}$ by 2, you get $\frac{1}{2}$.

Let's solve a problem:

$$\frac{}{8} = \frac{15}{40}$$

To solve the missing numerator, we can cross multiply.

$$40x = 8 \times 15$$

$$40x = 120$$

$$x = \frac{120}{40} = x = 3$$

$$\frac{3}{8} = \frac{15}{40}$$

Convert Fractions and Decimals

To transform a fraction into a decimal, we divide the numerator by the denominator.

For instance, $\frac{1}{4}$ equals 0.25 because when we divide 1 by 4, we get 0.25.

In certain cases, the resulting decimal repeats infinitely, like $\frac{1}{3}$, which equals 0.3333...
In such instances, we round the decimal to a specific number of decimal places.

Let's solve a problem:

$$\frac{52}{100} = \underline{0.52}$$

Least Common Multiple (LCM)

The Lowest Common Multiple (LCM) of two or more numbers is the smallest multiple that is divisible by each of the numbers.

There are several methods to find the LCM; however, we will focus on only two:

Listing Multiples: List the multiples of each number until you find a common multiple. For example:

$$8 \quad \underline{8,\ 16,\ 24,\ 32,\ 40,\ 48,\ 56}$$
$$7 \quad \underline{7,\ 14,\ 21,\ 28,\ 35,\ 42,\ 49,\ 56}\ ,\ \text{LCM} = \underline{56}$$

Division Method: Divide each number with the smallest prime number that divides at least one of the numbers evenly. The product of all the divisors and quotients is the LCM. For example:

2	7	8
2	7	4
2	7	2
7	7	1
	1	1

$$\text{LCM} = 2 \times 2 \times 2 \times 7 = \underline{56}$$

Both methods have their advantages. For big numbers, using the division way is usually faster. But if we are working with smaller numbers or like seeing patterns, listing multiples might make more sense.

Fractions Multiplication

To multiply fractions, we simply multiply the numerators together to get the new numerator and multiply the denominators together to get the new denominator.

For example, let's multiply: $\frac{2}{4} \times \frac{1}{4}$

$$\text{Numerator: } 2 \times 1 = 2$$

$$\text{Denominator: } 4 \times 4 = 16$$

$$\text{Therefore, } \frac{2}{16}$$

$$\text{we can simplify the resulting fraction: } \frac{1}{8}$$

Let's solve a problem:

$$\frac{4}{5} \times \frac{4}{5} = \frac{4 \times 4}{5 \times 5} = \frac{16}{25}$$

Fractions Division

To divide fractions, we multiply by the reciprocal of the divisor.

For example, let's divide:

$$\frac{6}{8} \div \frac{4}{8}$$

$$\frac{6}{8} \times \frac{8}{4} = \frac{48}{32} = \frac{3}{2}$$

<u>Mixed Numbers: Mixed into Improper</u>

Mixed numbers and improper fractions are two different ways to represent the same value of a fraction.

1. **Mixed Number:** A mixed number is a combination of a whole number and a proper fraction. For example, $2\frac{1}{3}$ is a mixed number, where 2 is the whole number part and $\frac{1}{3}$ is the fraction part.

2. **Improper Fraction:** An improper fraction is a fraction where the numerator is greater than or equal to the denominator. For example, $\frac{7}{3}$ is an improper fraction because 6 is greater than 3.

To convert a mixed number to an improper fraction, you multiply the whole number by the denominator of the fraction, add the numerator, and then write the result over the original denominator. For example:

$$2\frac{1}{3} = \frac{2 \times 3 + 1}{3} = \frac{7}{3}$$

To convert an improper fraction to a mixed number, we divide the numerator by the denominator. The quotient becomes the whole number part, and the remainder becomes the numerator of the fraction. For example:

$$\frac{7}{3} = 2\frac{1}{3}$$

Let's solve some problems:

$$2\frac{10}{20} = \frac{\begin{array}{l}20 \times 2 = 40\\ 40 + 10 = 50\end{array}}{} = \frac{50}{20} = \frac{5}{2}$$

$$\frac{41}{16} = \frac{2\frac{9}{16}}{}$$

$$41 \div 16 = 2 \text{ with a remainder of } 9$$

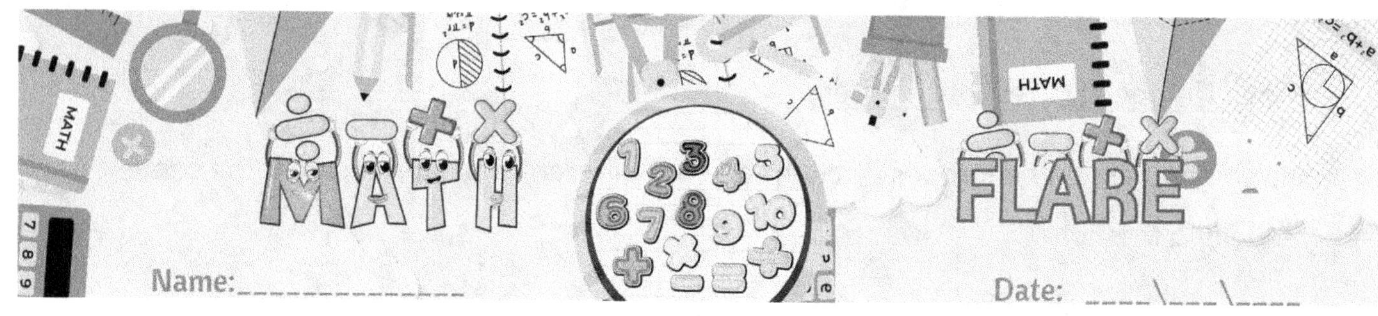

Equivalent Fractions

1. $\dfrac{5}{7} = \dfrac{40}{} = \dfrac{15}{}$

2. $\dfrac{9}{19} = \dfrac{}{133} = \dfrac{}{152}$

3. $\dfrac{3}{5} = \dfrac{30}{} = \dfrac{9}{}$

4. $\dfrac{1}{3} = \dfrac{7}{} = \dfrac{9}{}$

5. $\dfrac{5}{6} = \dfrac{30}{} = \dfrac{}{42}$

6. $\dfrac{6}{17} = \dfrac{}{85} = \dfrac{24}{}$

7. $\dfrac{8}{14} = \dfrac{}{84} = \dfrac{}{42}$

8. $\dfrac{1}{2} = \dfrac{}{6} = \dfrac{}{4}$

9. $\dfrac{15}{16} = \dfrac{150}{} = \dfrac{}{128}$

10. $\dfrac{12}{18} = \dfrac{36}{} = \dfrac{}{180}$

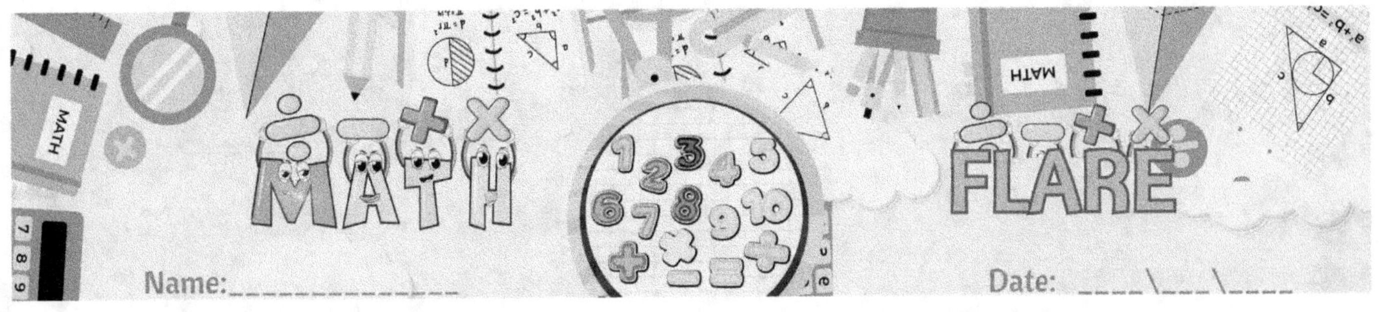

11. $\dfrac{9}{15} = \dfrac{36}{} = \dfrac{45}{}$

12. $\dfrac{11}{13} = \dfrac{22}{} = \dfrac{}{52}$

13. $\dfrac{7}{12} = \dfrac{70}{} = \dfrac{}{72}$

14. $\dfrac{9}{11} = \dfrac{}{99} = \dfrac{}{110}$

15. $\dfrac{3}{4} = \dfrac{24}{} = \dfrac{18}{}$

16. $\dfrac{8}{9} = \dfrac{32}{} = \dfrac{16}{}$

17. $\dfrac{8}{20} = \dfrac{}{80} = \dfrac{}{200}$

18. $\dfrac{1}{2} = \dfrac{2}{} = \dfrac{3}{}$

19. $\dfrac{3}{11} = \dfrac{}{110} = \dfrac{}{44}$

20. $\dfrac{16}{17} = \dfrac{}{136} = \dfrac{}{68}$

21. $\dfrac{11}{14} = \dfrac{}{42} = \dfrac{22}{}$

22. $\dfrac{5}{6} = \dfrac{}{54} = \dfrac{25}{}$

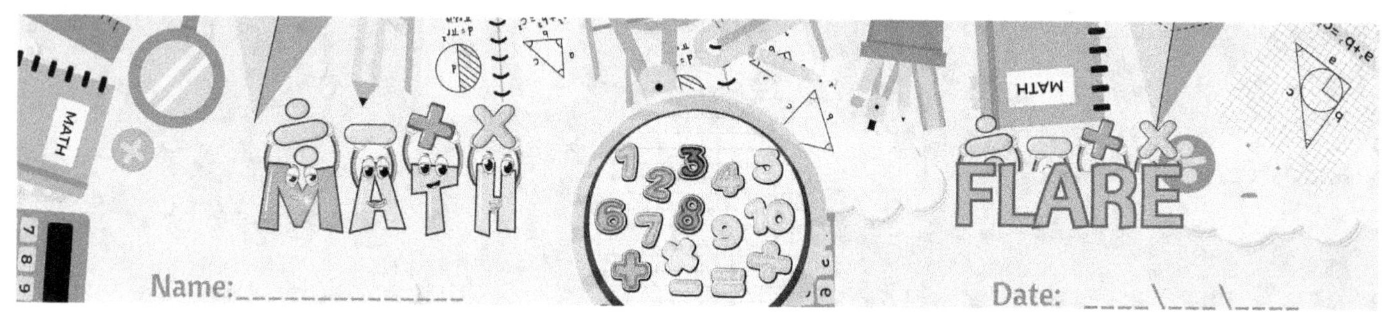

23. $\dfrac{2}{7} = \dfrac{16}{} = \dfrac{6}{}$

24. $\dfrac{2}{18} = \dfrac{8}{} = \dfrac{}{126}$

25. $\dfrac{7}{9} = \dfrac{}{36} = \dfrac{}{90}$

26. $\dfrac{16}{19} = \dfrac{}{152} = \dfrac{}{190}$

27. $\dfrac{2}{13} = \dfrac{6}{} = \dfrac{}{52}$

28. $\dfrac{15}{20} = \dfrac{}{40} = \dfrac{}{80}$

29. $\dfrac{2}{3} = \dfrac{16}{} = \dfrac{10}{}$

30. $\dfrac{6}{15} = \dfrac{}{75} = \dfrac{54}{}$

31. $\dfrac{1}{5} = \dfrac{9}{} = \dfrac{}{40}$

32. $\dfrac{1}{4} = \dfrac{}{12} = \dfrac{4}{}$

33. $\dfrac{7}{12} = \dfrac{21}{} = \dfrac{14}{}$

34. $\dfrac{6}{8} = \dfrac{}{72} = \dfrac{60}{}$

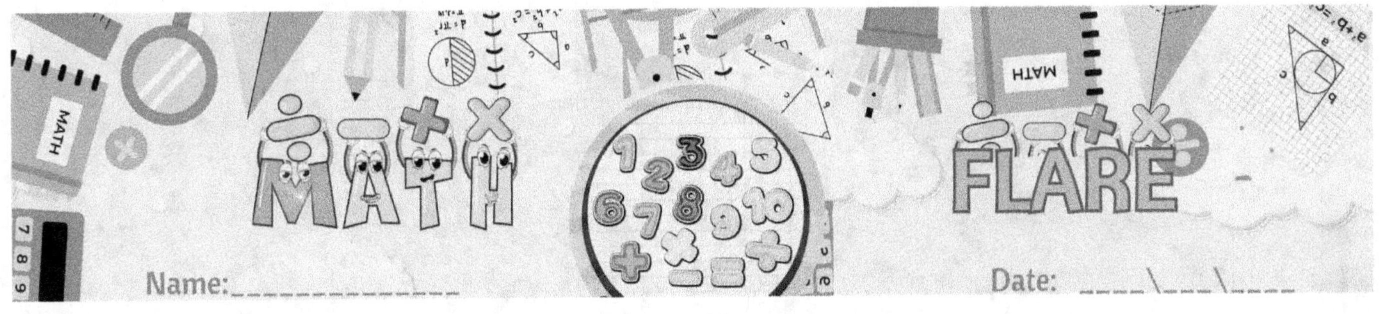

35. $\dfrac{2}{16} = \dfrac{}{96} = \dfrac{}{128}$

36. $\dfrac{6}{10} = \dfrac{}{30} = \dfrac{24}{}$

37. $\dfrac{1}{6} = \dfrac{3}{} = \dfrac{10}{}$

38. $\dfrac{7}{12} = \dfrac{21}{} = \dfrac{}{60}$

39. $\dfrac{2}{5} = \dfrac{12}{} = \dfrac{}{20}$

40. $\dfrac{12}{20} = \dfrac{96}{} = \dfrac{}{120}$

41. $\dfrac{1}{3} = \dfrac{}{21} = \dfrac{3}{}$

42. $\dfrac{2}{8} = \dfrac{4}{} = \dfrac{}{56}$

43. $\dfrac{10}{19} = \dfrac{100}{} = \dfrac{30}{}$

44. $\dfrac{7}{15} = \dfrac{63}{} = \dfrac{}{75}$

45. $\dfrac{5}{14} = \dfrac{}{84} = \dfrac{}{56}$

46. $\dfrac{6}{7} = \dfrac{}{35} = \dfrac{}{56}$

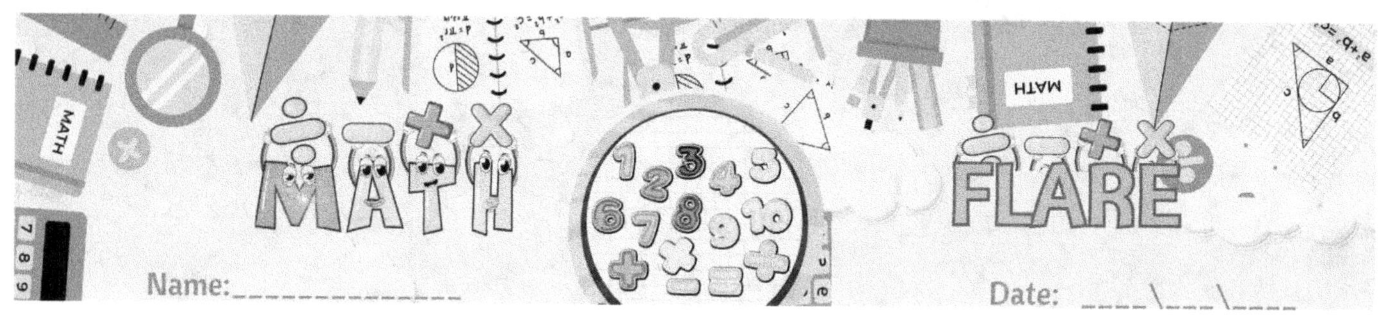

47. $\dfrac{15}{17} = \dfrac{60}{} = \dfrac{}{119}$

48. $\dfrac{4}{13} = \dfrac{}{117} = \dfrac{}{26}$

49. $\dfrac{2}{4} = \dfrac{12}{} = \dfrac{}{20}$

50. $\dfrac{7}{18} = \dfrac{35}{} = \dfrac{21}{}$

51. $\dfrac{12}{16} = \dfrac{48}{} = \dfrac{}{160}$

52. $\dfrac{2}{11} = \dfrac{20}{} = \dfrac{}{44}$

53. $\dfrac{6}{9} = \dfrac{42}{} = \dfrac{}{18}$

54. $\dfrac{6}{10} = \dfrac{}{90} = \dfrac{}{70}$

55. $\dfrac{1}{2} = \dfrac{}{6} = \dfrac{}{8}$

56. $\dfrac{1}{2} = \dfrac{7}{} = \dfrac{2}{}$

57. $\dfrac{2}{15} = \dfrac{6}{} = \dfrac{}{105}$

58. $\dfrac{5}{10} = \dfrac{}{20} = \dfrac{50}{}$

Fractions Addition: Uncommon Denominator

Find the sum.

1. $\dfrac{3}{5} + \dfrac{1}{8} =$ _______________

2. $\dfrac{3}{10} + \dfrac{1}{2} =$ _______________

3. $\dfrac{1}{14} + \dfrac{9}{16} =$ _______________

4. $\dfrac{8}{16} + \dfrac{4}{15} =$ _______________

5. $\dfrac{3}{10} + \dfrac{2}{8} =$ _______________

6. $\dfrac{4}{6} + \dfrac{1}{19} =$ _______________

7. $\dfrac{8}{15} + \dfrac{4}{14} =$ _______________

8. $\dfrac{1}{4} + \dfrac{4}{12} =$ _______________

9. $\dfrac{4}{7} + \dfrac{1}{7} =$ _______________

10. $\dfrac{4}{9} + \dfrac{3}{10} =$ _______________

11. $\dfrac{4}{11} + \dfrac{1}{5} =$ _______________

12. $\dfrac{3}{8} + \dfrac{5}{20} =$ _______________

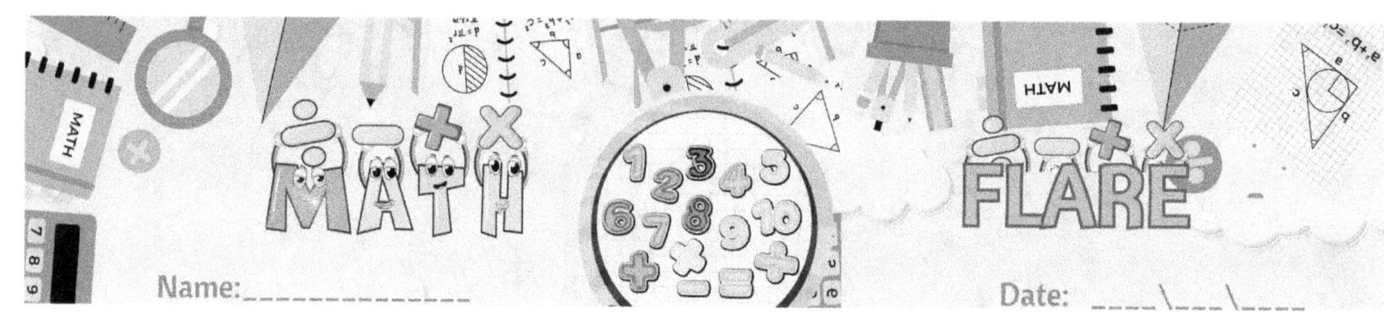

13. $\dfrac{2}{18} + \dfrac{3}{6} =$ _______________

14. $\dfrac{3}{5} + \dfrac{5}{20} =$ _______________

15. $\dfrac{3}{13} + \dfrac{5}{9} =$ _______________

16. $\dfrac{3}{11} + \dfrac{2}{12} =$ _______________

17. $\dfrac{1}{2} + \dfrac{1}{7} =$ _______________

18. $\dfrac{1}{20} + \dfrac{6}{14} =$ _______________

19. $\dfrac{6}{15} + \dfrac{6}{17} =$ _______________

20. $\dfrac{11}{18} + \dfrac{2}{15} =$ _______________

21. $\dfrac{2}{9} + \dfrac{1}{2} =$ _______________

22. $\dfrac{5}{16} + \dfrac{4}{19} =$ _______________

23. $\dfrac{2}{9} + \dfrac{1}{3} =$ _______________

24. $\dfrac{1}{6} + \dfrac{7}{15} =$ _______________

25. $\dfrac{3}{20} + \dfrac{5}{17} =$ _______________

26. $\dfrac{1}{2} + \dfrac{3}{14} =$ _______________

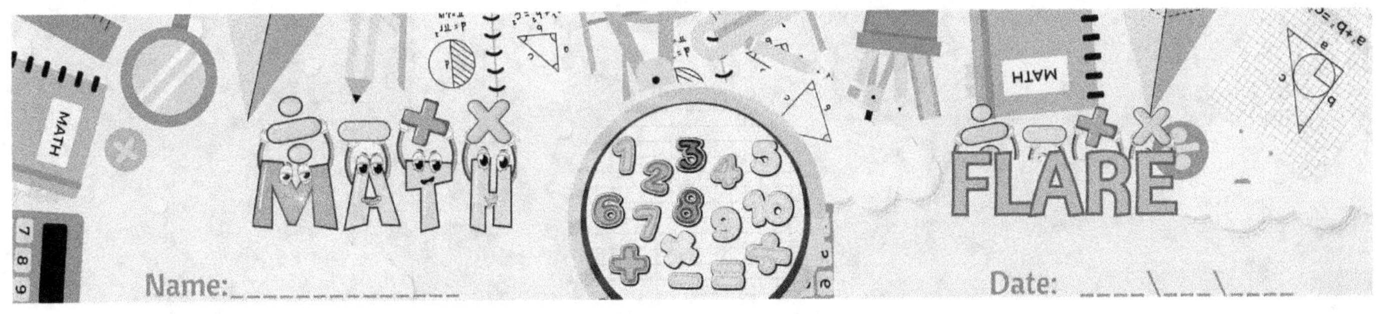

27. $\dfrac{5}{19} + \dfrac{3}{8} =$ ______________

28. $\dfrac{6}{11} + \dfrac{7}{16} =$ ______________

29. $\dfrac{2}{4} + \dfrac{7}{20} =$ ______________

30. $\dfrac{3}{15} + \dfrac{3}{11} =$ ______________

31. $\dfrac{2}{16} + \dfrac{1}{2} =$ ______________

32. $\dfrac{4}{10} + \dfrac{6}{11} =$ ______________

33. $\dfrac{9}{16} + \dfrac{1}{5} =$ ______________

34. $\dfrac{9}{19} + \dfrac{2}{16} =$ ______________

35. $\dfrac{2}{3} + \dfrac{3}{13} =$ ______________

36. $\dfrac{1}{10} + \dfrac{10}{17} =$ ______________

37. $\dfrac{4}{11} + \dfrac{1}{6} =$ ______________

38. $\dfrac{1}{9} + \dfrac{3}{12} =$ ______________

39. $\dfrac{2}{20} + \dfrac{8}{15} =$ ______________

40. $\dfrac{7}{12} + \dfrac{3}{19} =$ ______________

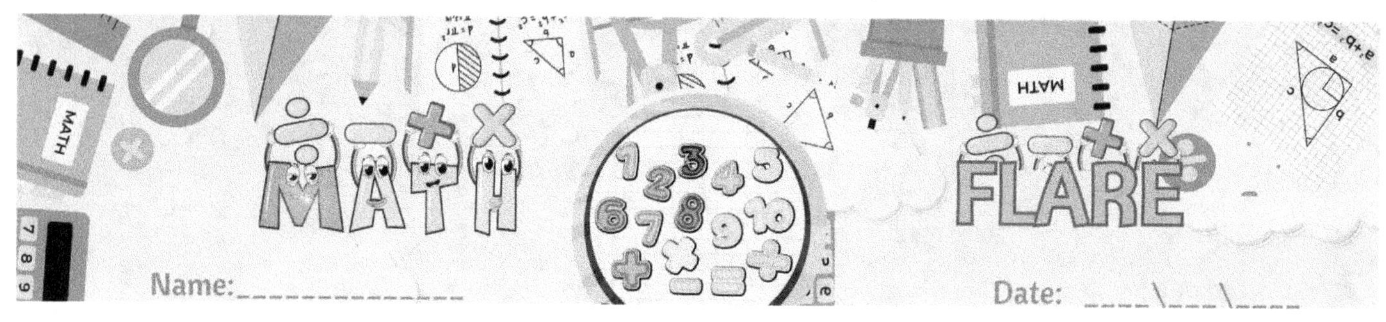

41. $\dfrac{3}{7} + \dfrac{1}{14} =$ _________________

42. $\dfrac{2}{11} + \dfrac{4}{13} =$ _________________

43. $\dfrac{1}{7} + \dfrac{4}{16} =$ _________________

44. $\dfrac{1}{6} + \dfrac{9}{12} =$ _________________

45. $\dfrac{2}{3} + \dfrac{5}{18} =$ _________________

46. $\dfrac{5}{10} + \dfrac{2}{7} =$ _________________

47. $\dfrac{1}{17} + \dfrac{6}{9} =$ _________________

48. $\dfrac{4}{13} + \dfrac{1}{4} =$ _________________

49. $\dfrac{9}{12} + \dfrac{1}{8} =$ _________________

50. $\dfrac{5}{16} + \dfrac{1}{2} =$ _________________

51. $\dfrac{6}{9} + \dfrac{1}{10} =$ _________________

52. $\dfrac{9}{15} + \dfrac{3}{15} =$ _________________

53. $\dfrac{5}{10} + \dfrac{1}{7} =$ _________________

54. $\dfrac{1}{2} + \dfrac{1}{6} =$ _________________

55. $\dfrac{5}{7} + \dfrac{1}{4} =$ _______________

56. $\dfrac{3}{5} + \dfrac{2}{19} =$ _______________

57. $\dfrac{2}{16} + \dfrac{4}{5} =$ _______________

58. $\dfrac{7}{11} + \dfrac{1}{3} =$ _______________

59. $\dfrac{9}{20} + \dfrac{10}{20} =$ _______________

60. $\dfrac{11}{17} + \dfrac{4}{14} =$ _______________

61. $\dfrac{5}{15} + \dfrac{1}{9} =$ _______________

62. $\dfrac{5}{16} + \dfrac{7}{11} =$ _______________

63. $\dfrac{2}{7} + \dfrac{2}{3} =$ _______________

64. $\dfrac{11}{19} + \dfrac{2}{15} =$ _______________

65. $\dfrac{7}{8} + \dfrac{2}{20} =$ _______________

66. $\dfrac{7}{17} + \dfrac{4}{7} =$ _______________

67. $\dfrac{2}{20} + \dfrac{2}{4} =$ _______________

68. $\dfrac{1}{2} + \dfrac{5}{14} =$ _______________

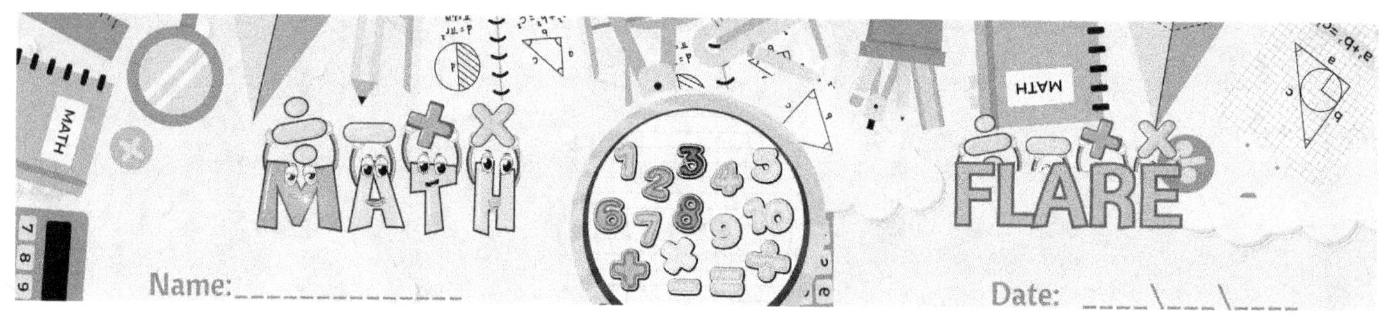

69. $\frac{10}{14} + \frac{1}{10} =$ ________________

70. $\frac{1}{4} + \frac{9}{18} =$ ________________

71. $\frac{2}{16} + \frac{8}{12} =$ ________________

72. $\frac{1}{2} + \frac{1}{11} =$ ________________

73. $\frac{8}{15} + \frac{2}{5} =$ ________________

74. $\frac{6}{11} + \frac{2}{16} =$ ________________

75. $\frac{1}{10} + \frac{4}{17} =$ ________________

76. $\frac{2}{7} + \frac{1}{3} =$ ________________

77. $\frac{8}{17} + \frac{2}{4} =$ ________________

78. $\frac{3}{14} + \frac{1}{9} =$ ________________

79. $\frac{12}{18} + \frac{2}{10} =$ ________________

80. $\frac{6}{19} + \frac{4}{9} =$ ________________

81. $\frac{1}{10} + \frac{11}{17} =$ ________________

82. $\frac{1}{9} + \frac{1}{3} =$ ________________

83. $\dfrac{2}{5} + \dfrac{1}{7} =$ ______________

84. $\dfrac{2}{7} + \dfrac{10}{15} =$ ______________

85. $\dfrac{1}{14} + \dfrac{3}{6} =$ ______________

86. $\dfrac{7}{11} + \dfrac{1}{11} =$ ______________

87. $\dfrac{1}{6} + \dfrac{5}{10} =$ ______________

88. $\dfrac{3}{4} + \dfrac{1}{19} =$ ______________

89. $\dfrac{11}{16} + \dfrac{3}{10} =$ ______________

90. $\dfrac{1}{10} + \dfrac{1}{5} =$ ______________

91. $\dfrac{3}{20} + \dfrac{4}{6} =$ ______________

92. $\dfrac{6}{11} + \dfrac{1}{12} =$ ______________

93. $\dfrac{3}{6} + \dfrac{2}{8} =$ ______________

94. $\dfrac{8}{19} + \dfrac{8}{15} =$ ______________

95. $\dfrac{9}{18} + \dfrac{1}{3} =$ ______________

96. $\dfrac{1}{16} + \dfrac{2}{13} =$ ______________

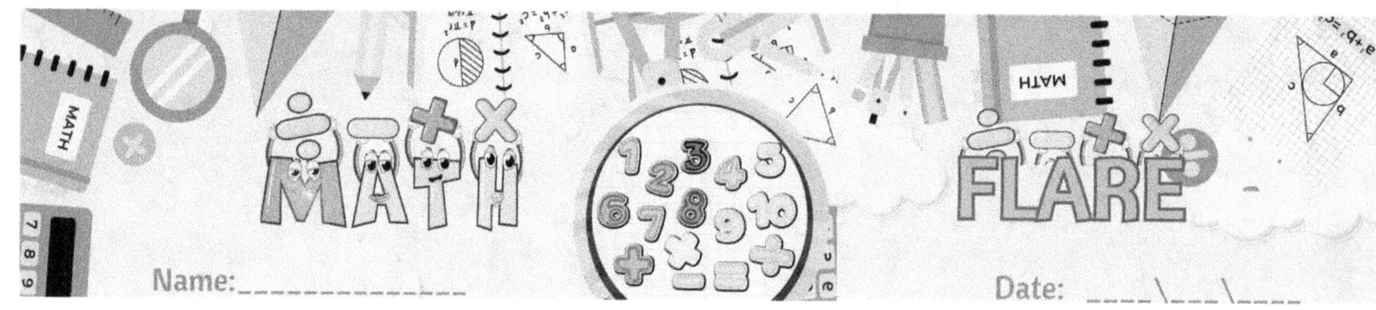

Fractions Subtraction - Uncommon Denominator

Find the difference.

1. $\dfrac{8}{14} - \dfrac{2}{15} =$ ______________

2. $\dfrac{3}{8} - \dfrac{1}{20} =$ ______________

3. $\dfrac{1}{2} - \dfrac{1}{4} =$ ______________

4. $\dfrac{12}{20} - \dfrac{4}{7} =$ ______________

5. $\dfrac{2}{4} - \dfrac{1}{18} =$ ______________

6. $\dfrac{5}{19} - \dfrac{3}{12} =$ ______________

7. $\dfrac{10}{13} - \dfrac{1}{18} =$ ______________

8. $\dfrac{9}{12} - \dfrac{5}{10} =$ ______________

9. $\dfrac{6}{14} - \dfrac{2}{9} =$ ______________

10. $\dfrac{4}{6} - \dfrac{7}{17} =$ ______________

11. $\dfrac{9}{11} - \dfrac{12}{16} =$ ______________

12. $\dfrac{14}{18} - \dfrac{1}{19} =$ ______________

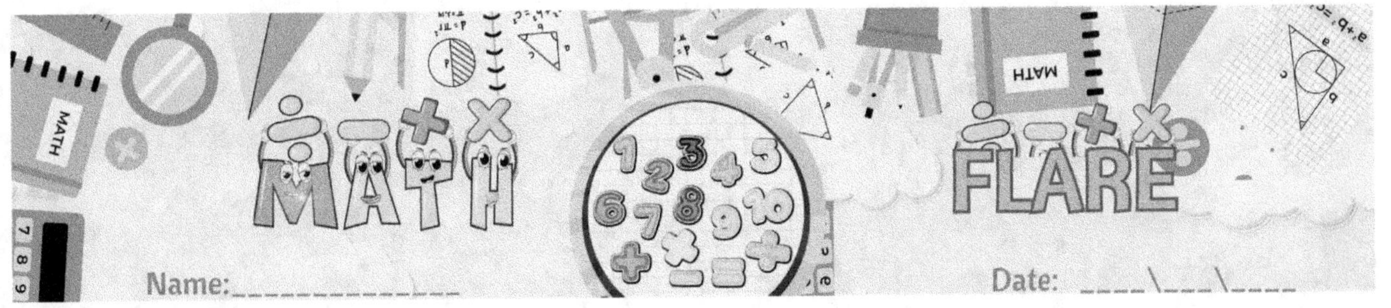

13. $\dfrac{7}{12} - \dfrac{6}{14} =$ _______________

14. $\dfrac{15}{20} - \dfrac{1}{3} =$ _______________

15. $\dfrac{8}{9} - \dfrac{6}{13} =$ _______________

16. $\dfrac{6}{17} - \dfrac{3}{10} =$ _______________

17. $\dfrac{4}{7} - \dfrac{2}{6} =$ _______________

18. $\dfrac{18}{19} - \dfrac{1}{14} =$ _______________

19. $\dfrac{10}{11} - \dfrac{1}{3} =$ _______________

20. $\dfrac{12}{15} - \dfrac{1}{7} =$ _______________

21. $\dfrac{18}{20} - \dfrac{12}{16} =$ _______________

22. $\dfrac{3}{5} - \dfrac{1}{5} =$ _______________

23. $\dfrac{7}{13} - \dfrac{3}{13} =$ _______________

24. $\dfrac{3}{4} - \dfrac{11}{17} =$ _______________

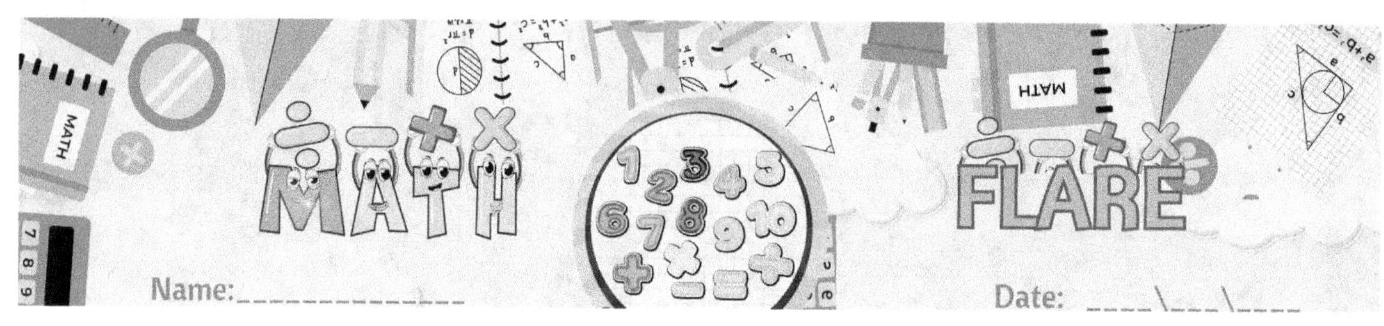

25. $\dfrac{1}{2} - \dfrac{3}{14} =$ _______________

26. $\dfrac{5}{12} - \dfrac{3}{11} =$ _______________

27. $\dfrac{8}{10} - \dfrac{4}{10} =$ _______________

28. $\dfrac{3}{5} - \dfrac{1}{3} =$ _______________

29. $\dfrac{10}{14} - \dfrac{1}{2} =$ _______________

30. $\dfrac{3}{6} - \dfrac{3}{11} =$ _______________

31. $\dfrac{5}{13} - \dfrac{1}{7} =$ _______________

32. $\dfrac{5}{15} - \dfrac{2}{10} =$ _______________

33. $\dfrac{5}{9} - \dfrac{5}{15} =$ _______________

34. $\dfrac{10}{15} - \dfrac{9}{14} =$ _______________

35. $\dfrac{1}{2} - \dfrac{1}{9} =$ _______________

36. $\dfrac{10}{19} - \dfrac{2}{4} =$ _______________

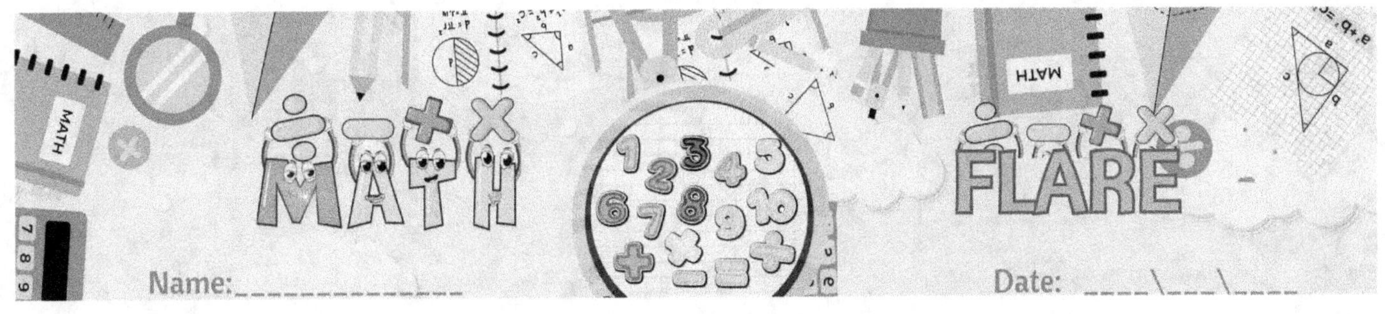

37. $\dfrac{10}{19} - \dfrac{1}{14} =$ _______________

38. $\dfrac{6}{7} - \dfrac{6}{10} =$ _______________

39. $\dfrac{6}{15} - \dfrac{4}{16} =$ _______________

40. $\dfrac{5}{6} - \dfrac{4}{5} =$ _______________

41. $\dfrac{9}{12} - \dfrac{3}{13} =$ _______________

42. $\dfrac{7}{16} - \dfrac{5}{18} =$ _______________

43. $\dfrac{11}{20} - \dfrac{1}{9} =$ _______________

44. $\dfrac{8}{10} - \dfrac{4}{11} =$ _______________

45. $\dfrac{12}{18} - \dfrac{1}{3} =$ _______________

46. $\dfrac{2}{4} - \dfrac{2}{5} =$ _______________

47. $\dfrac{7}{12} - \dfrac{4}{18} =$ _______________

48. $\dfrac{4}{13} - \dfrac{1}{12} =$ _______________

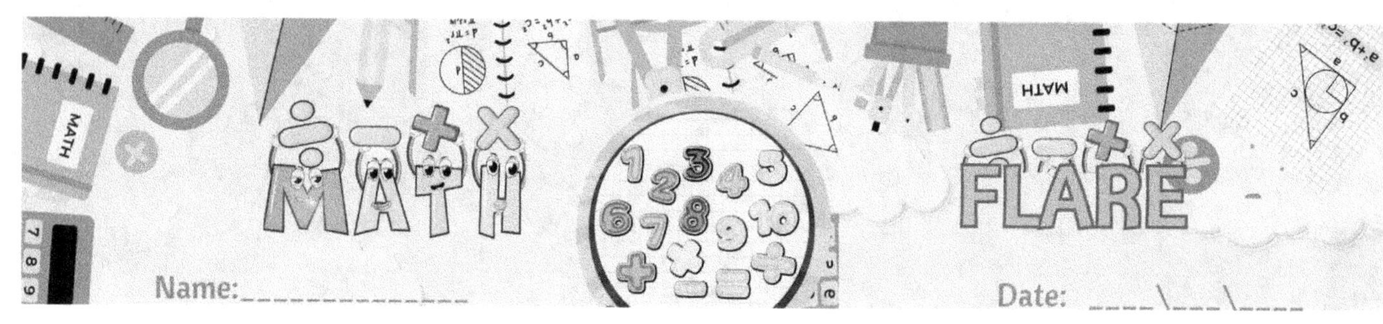

49. $\dfrac{14}{16} - \dfrac{8}{11} =$ __________

50. $\dfrac{17}{18} - \dfrac{8}{14} =$ __________

51. $\dfrac{16}{17} - \dfrac{1}{9} =$ __________

52. $\dfrac{8}{11} - \dfrac{12}{17} =$ __________

53. $\dfrac{5}{10} - \dfrac{2}{8} =$ __________

54. $\dfrac{11}{15} - \dfrac{1}{4} =$ __________

55. $\dfrac{3}{4} - \dfrac{1}{3} =$ __________

56. $\dfrac{8}{16} - \dfrac{4}{19} =$ __________

57. $\dfrac{3}{4} - \dfrac{1}{2} =$ __________

58. $\dfrac{6}{8} - \dfrac{2}{4} =$ __________

59. $\dfrac{13}{19} - \dfrac{2}{16} =$ __________

60. $\dfrac{4}{5} - \dfrac{5}{11} =$ __________

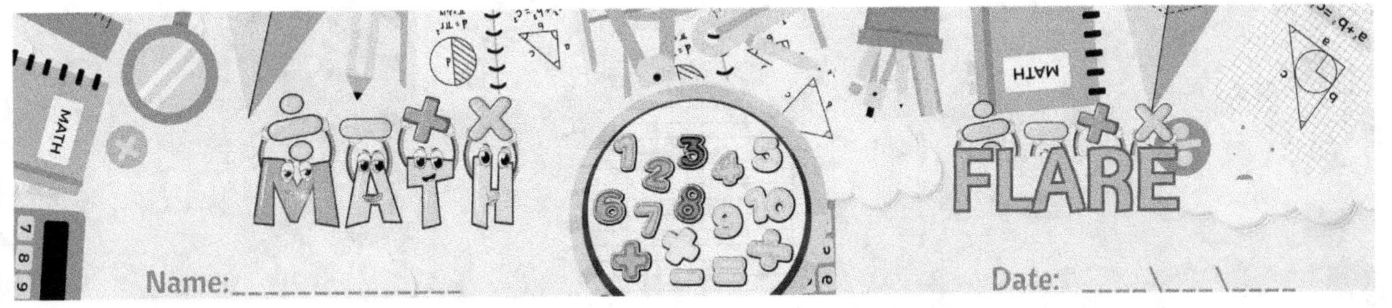

61. $\dfrac{1}{4} - \dfrac{1}{13} =$ ________________

62. $\dfrac{4}{10} - \dfrac{7}{20} =$ ________________

63. $\dfrac{12}{18} - \dfrac{1}{17} =$ ________________

64. $\dfrac{8}{16} - \dfrac{1}{3} =$ ________________

65. $\dfrac{6}{9} - \dfrac{4}{19} =$ ________________

66. $\dfrac{4}{10} - \dfrac{2}{16} =$ ________________

67. $\dfrac{8}{12} - \dfrac{1}{11} =$ ________________

68. $\dfrac{5}{8} - \dfrac{3}{18} =$ ________________

69. $\dfrac{8}{13} - \dfrac{2}{8} =$ ________________

70. $\dfrac{13}{18} - \dfrac{2}{19} =$ ________________

71. $\dfrac{1}{2} - \dfrac{5}{16} =$ ________________

72. $\dfrac{16}{19} - \dfrac{1}{3} =$ ________________

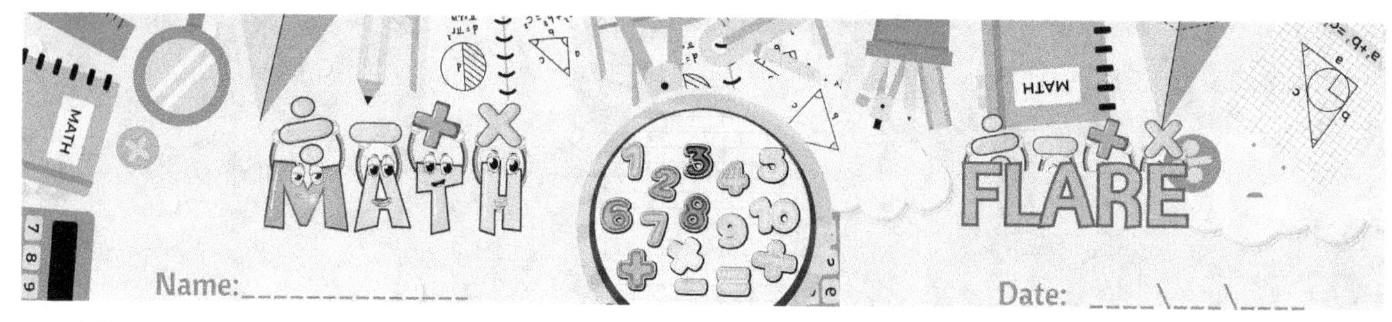

73. $\dfrac{7}{17} - \dfrac{1}{17} =$ _______________

74. $\dfrac{15}{20} - \dfrac{4}{14} =$ _______________

75. $\dfrac{1}{2} - \dfrac{2}{9} =$ _______________

76. $\dfrac{3}{9} - \dfrac{1}{4} =$ _______________

77. $\dfrac{7}{16} - \dfrac{3}{10} =$ _______________

78. $\dfrac{8}{12} - \dfrac{3}{18} =$ _______________

79. $\dfrac{5}{13} - \dfrac{2}{12} =$ _______________

80. $\dfrac{4}{5} - \dfrac{1}{8} =$ _______________

81. $\dfrac{1}{4} - \dfrac{2}{17} =$ _______________

82. $\dfrac{8}{13} - \dfrac{1}{2} =$ _______________

83. $\dfrac{7}{10} - \dfrac{6}{15} =$ _______________

84. $\dfrac{2}{8} - \dfrac{1}{7} =$ _______________

MathFlare - Fractions 4th and 5th Grade

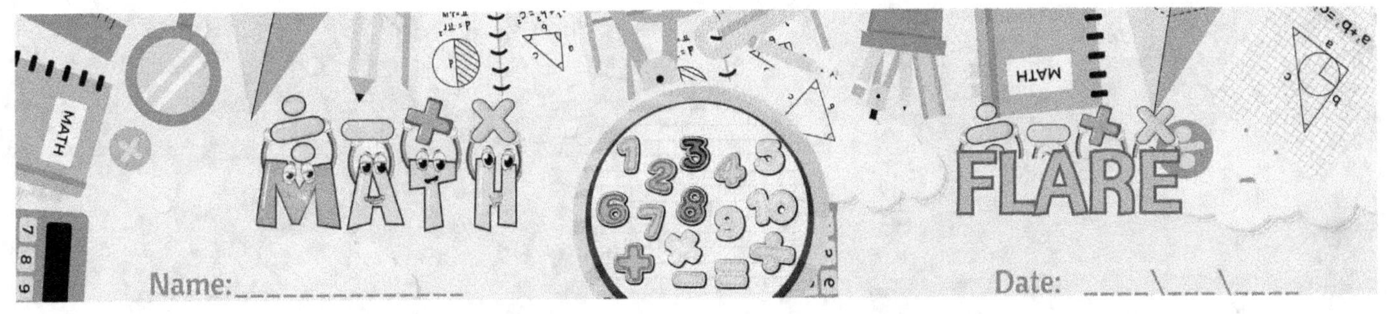

85. $\dfrac{9}{11} - \dfrac{6}{11} =$ _______________

86. $\dfrac{12}{18} - \dfrac{10}{19} =$ _______________

87. $\dfrac{13}{17} - \dfrac{3}{18} =$ _______________

88. $\dfrac{2}{3} - \dfrac{1}{4} =$ _______________

89. $\dfrac{8}{15} - \dfrac{5}{17} =$ _______________

90. $\dfrac{5}{17} - \dfrac{1}{6} =$ _______________

91. $\dfrac{16}{19} - \dfrac{5}{14} =$ _______________

92. $\dfrac{7}{8} - \dfrac{16}{20} =$ _______________

93. $\dfrac{3}{4} - \dfrac{5}{16} =$ _______________

94. $\dfrac{3}{5} - \dfrac{2}{4} =$ _______________

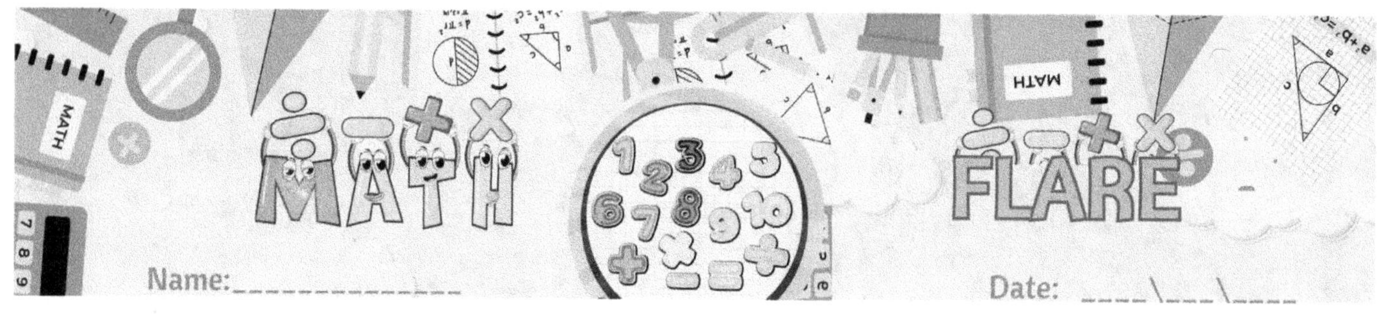

Fractions Multiplication

Find the product.

1. $\dfrac{1}{2} \times \dfrac{1}{9} =$ _______________

2. $\dfrac{14}{15} \times \dfrac{3}{4} =$ _______________

3. $\dfrac{5}{6} \times \dfrac{1}{2} =$ _______________

4. $\dfrac{2}{5} \times \dfrac{11}{14} =$ _______________

5. $\dfrac{2}{3} \times \dfrac{2}{3} =$ _______________

6. $\dfrac{4}{5} \times \dfrac{5}{11} =$ _______________

7. $\dfrac{6}{7} \times \dfrac{2}{13} =$ _______________

8. $\dfrac{7}{12} \times \dfrac{4}{5} =$ _______________

9. $\dfrac{3}{8} \times \dfrac{3}{4} =$ _______________

10. $\dfrac{3}{5} \times \dfrac{3}{7} =$ _______________

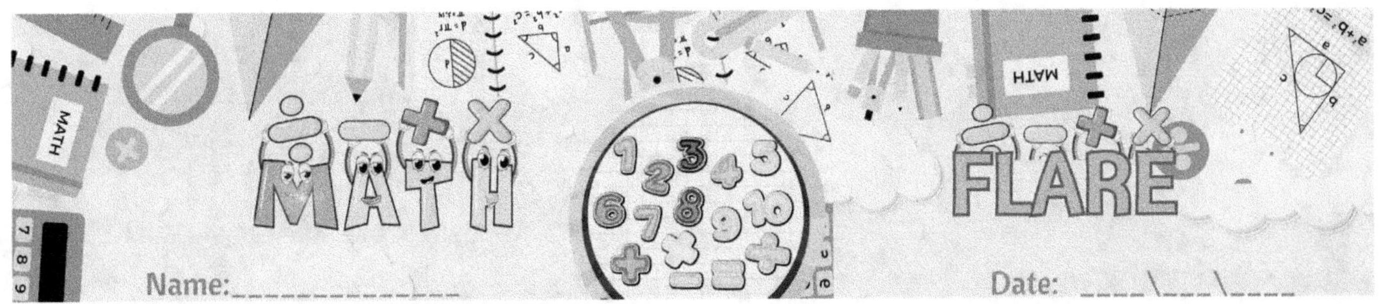

11. $\dfrac{1}{3} \times \dfrac{4}{5} =$ _______________

12. $\dfrac{2}{5} \times \dfrac{11}{13} =$ _______________

13. $\dfrac{10}{11} \times \dfrac{3}{4} =$ _______________

14. $\dfrac{7}{9} \times \dfrac{13}{14} =$ _______________

15. $\dfrac{3}{10} \times \dfrac{3}{16} =$ _______________

16. $\dfrac{1}{12} \times \dfrac{4}{15} =$ _______________

17. $\dfrac{1}{4} \times \dfrac{1}{3} =$ _______________

18. $\dfrac{2}{3} \times \dfrac{1}{2} =$ _______________

19. $\dfrac{1}{3} \times \dfrac{3}{7} =$ _______________

20. $\dfrac{1}{3} \times \dfrac{2}{3} =$ _______________

21. $\dfrac{9}{10} \times \dfrac{2}{15} =$ _______________

22. $\dfrac{6}{7} \times \dfrac{1}{4} =$ _______________

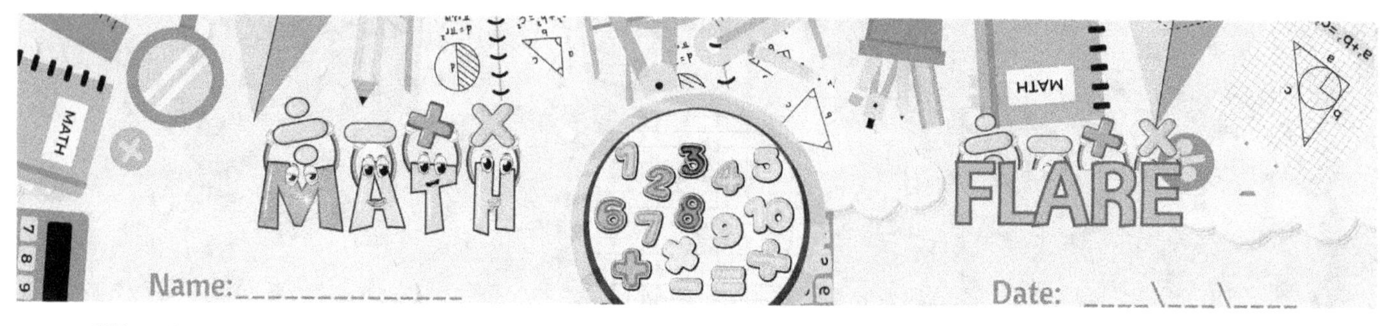

23. $\dfrac{6}{13} \times \dfrac{6}{11} =$ _________________

24. $\dfrac{1}{16} \times \dfrac{3}{5} =$ _________________

25. $\dfrac{1}{2} \times \dfrac{5}{12} =$ _________________

26. $\dfrac{2}{11} \times \dfrac{1}{3} =$ _________________

27. $\dfrac{5}{16} \times \dfrac{1}{3} =$ _________________

28. $\dfrac{1}{3} \times \dfrac{1}{2} =$ _________________

29. $\dfrac{5}{8} \times \dfrac{1}{6} =$ _________________

30. $\dfrac{7}{10} \times \dfrac{13}{16} =$ _________________

31. $\dfrac{1}{3} \times \dfrac{4}{9} =$ _________________

32. $\dfrac{7}{15} \times \dfrac{8}{11} =$ _________________

33. $\dfrac{5}{8} \times \dfrac{4}{7} =$ _________________

34. $\dfrac{1}{3} \times \dfrac{8}{15} =$ _________________

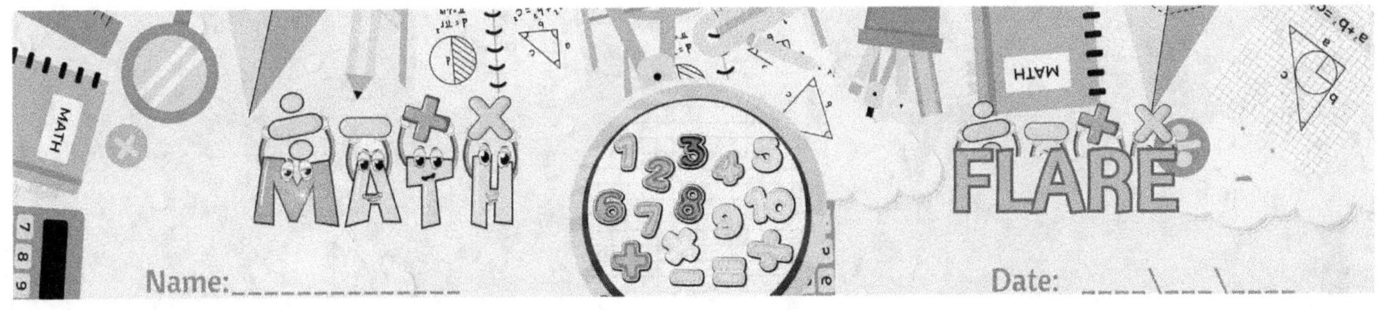

35. $\dfrac{3}{7} \times \dfrac{1}{2} =$ _______________

36. $\dfrac{1}{2} \times \dfrac{8}{9} =$ _______________

37. $\dfrac{5}{8} \times \dfrac{3}{5} =$ _______________

38. $\dfrac{1}{3} \times \dfrac{1}{4} =$ _______________

39. $\dfrac{1}{13} \times \dfrac{1}{6} =$ _______________

40. $\dfrac{5}{13} \times \dfrac{7}{16} =$ _______________

41. $\dfrac{1}{2} \times \dfrac{2}{7} =$ _______________

42. $\dfrac{2}{3} \times \dfrac{9}{10} =$ _______________

43. $\dfrac{15}{16} \times \dfrac{6}{7} =$ _______________

44. $\dfrac{13}{15} \times \dfrac{1}{2} =$ _______________

45. $\dfrac{3}{4} \times \dfrac{1}{5} =$ _______________

46. $\dfrac{6}{7} \times \dfrac{3}{13} =$ _______________

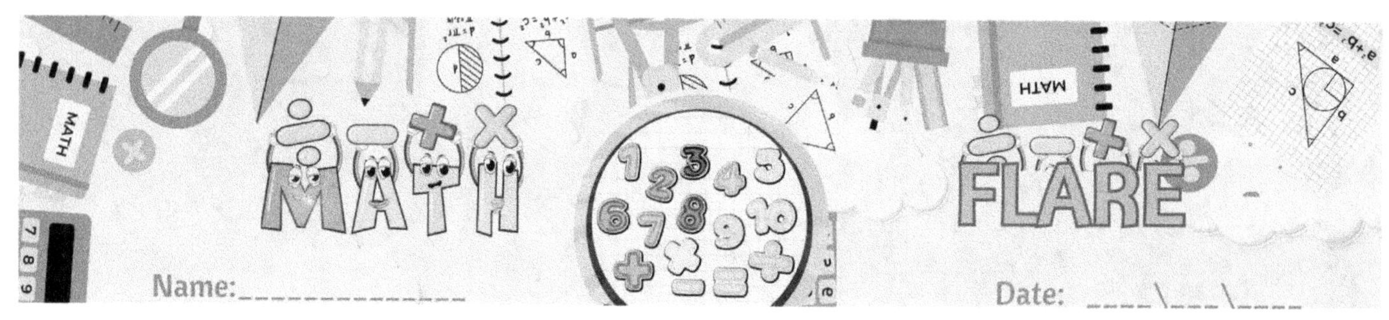

Name:________________ Date: ____________

47. $\dfrac{3}{5} \times \dfrac{5}{11} =$ _______________

48. $\dfrac{4}{5} \times \dfrac{1}{3} =$ _______________

49. $\dfrac{1}{2} \times \dfrac{1}{14} =$ _______________

50. $\dfrac{2}{3} \times \dfrac{4}{5} =$ _______________

51. $\dfrac{3}{14} \times \dfrac{1}{2} =$ _______________

52. $\dfrac{1}{4} \times \dfrac{1}{13} =$ _______________

53. $\dfrac{5}{6} \times \dfrac{1}{4} =$ _______________

54. $\dfrac{6}{11} \times \dfrac{3}{5} =$ _______________

55. $\dfrac{1}{2} \times \dfrac{1}{2} =$ _______________

56. $\dfrac{11}{15} \times \dfrac{2}{5} =$ _______________

57. $\dfrac{9}{11} \times \dfrac{11}{14} =$ _______________

58. $\dfrac{3}{5} \times \dfrac{9}{16} =$ _______________

59. $\dfrac{7}{9} \times \dfrac{7}{11} =$ _________________

60. $\dfrac{2}{3} \times \dfrac{3}{7} =$ _________________

61. $\dfrac{5}{8} \times \dfrac{1}{5} =$ _________________

62. $\dfrac{1}{4} \times \dfrac{3}{10} =$ _________________

63. $\dfrac{1}{5} \times \dfrac{1}{3} =$ _________________

64. $\dfrac{3}{5} \times \dfrac{1}{5} =$ _________________

65. $\dfrac{6}{13} \times \dfrac{1}{2} =$ _________________

66. $\dfrac{3}{11} \times \dfrac{1}{2} =$ _________________

67. $\dfrac{1}{7} \times \dfrac{5}{7} =$ _________________

68. $\dfrac{1}{14} \times \dfrac{3}{4} =$ _________________

69. $\dfrac{1}{3} \times \dfrac{1}{3} =$ _________________

70. $\dfrac{14}{15} \times \dfrac{3}{5} =$ _________________

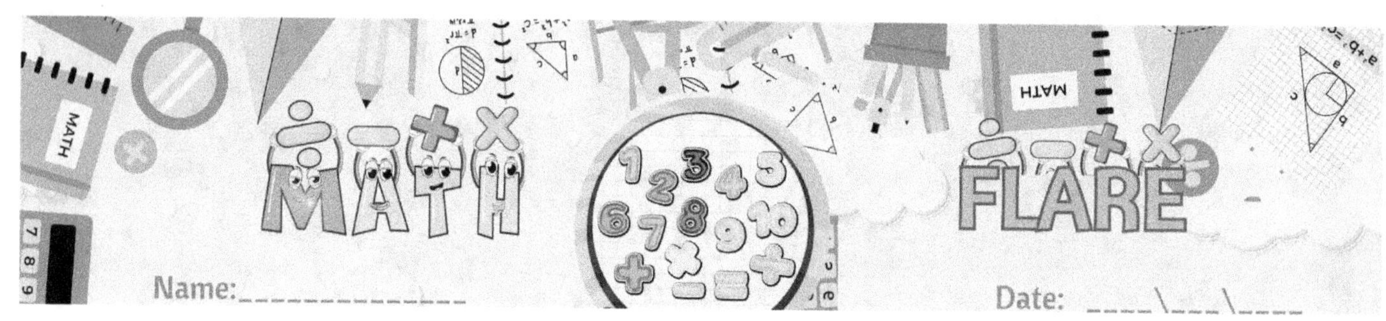

71. $\dfrac{3}{4} \times \dfrac{1}{2} =$ _______________

72. $\dfrac{1}{2} \times \dfrac{4}{11} =$ _______________

73. $\dfrac{1}{2} \times \dfrac{1}{5} =$ _______________

74. $\dfrac{9}{13} \times \dfrac{1}{9} =$ _______________

75. $\dfrac{2}{7} \times \dfrac{1}{2} =$ _______________

76. $\dfrac{1}{6} \times \dfrac{3}{5} =$ _______________

77. $\dfrac{11}{14} \times \dfrac{14}{15} =$ _______________

78. $\dfrac{13}{16} \times \dfrac{2}{3} =$ _______________

79. $\dfrac{1}{4} \times \dfrac{1}{4} =$ _______________

80. $\dfrac{1}{2} \times \dfrac{4}{5} =$ _______________

81. $\dfrac{8}{9} \times \dfrac{5}{12} =$ _______________

82. $\dfrac{1}{7} \times \dfrac{2}{7} =$ _______________

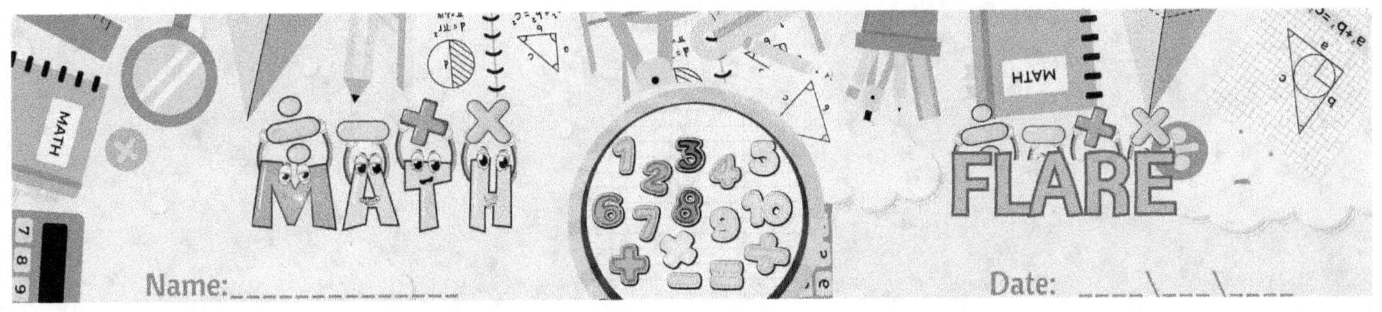

83. $\dfrac{1}{9} \times \dfrac{3}{8} =$ _______________

84. $\dfrac{7}{10} \times \dfrac{1}{12} =$ _______________

85. $\dfrac{9}{16} \times \dfrac{1}{14} =$ _______________

86. $\dfrac{6}{11} \times \dfrac{6}{7} =$ _______________

87. $\dfrac{3}{5} \times \dfrac{1}{2} =$ _______________

88. $\dfrac{1}{2} \times \dfrac{2}{5} =$ _______________

89. $\dfrac{5}{7} \times \dfrac{1}{2} =$ _______________

90. $\dfrac{7}{16} \times \dfrac{7}{15} =$ _______________

91. $\dfrac{2}{3} \times \dfrac{1}{3} =$ _______________

92. $\dfrac{7}{8} \times \dfrac{1}{3} =$ _______________

93. $\dfrac{2}{3} \times \dfrac{1}{7} =$ _______________

94. $\dfrac{2}{5} \times \dfrac{2}{9} =$ _______________

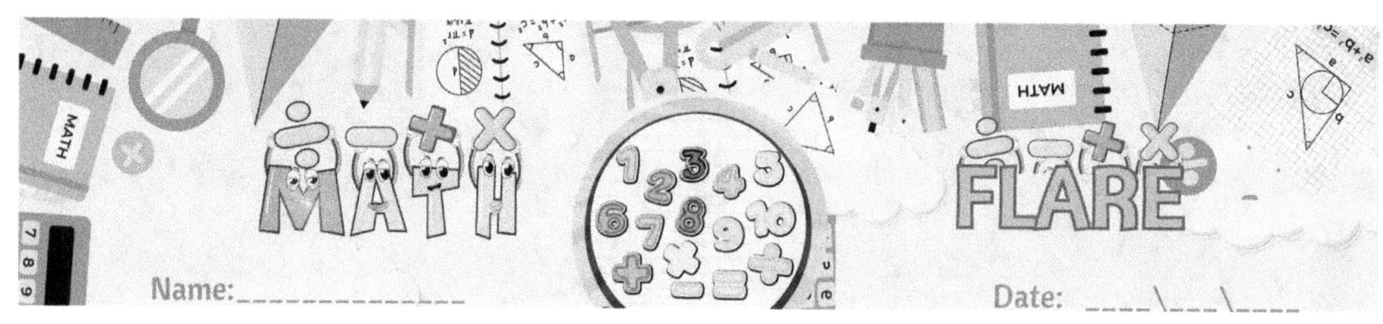

95. $\dfrac{3}{13} \times \dfrac{4}{13} =$ _______________

96. $\dfrac{1}{2} \times \dfrac{1}{3} =$ _______________

97. $\dfrac{1}{3} \times \dfrac{5}{8} =$ _______________

98. $\dfrac{5}{11} \times \dfrac{2}{7} =$ _______________

99. $\dfrac{3}{4} \times \dfrac{2}{3} =$ _______________

100. $\dfrac{3}{13} \times \dfrac{4}{5} =$ _______________

101. $\dfrac{9}{16} \times \dfrac{5}{6} =$ _______________

102. $\dfrac{14}{15} \times \dfrac{2}{9} =$ _______________

103. $\dfrac{4}{7} \times \dfrac{1}{3} =$ _______________

104. $\dfrac{1}{2} \times \dfrac{2}{3} =$ _______________

105. $\dfrac{1}{2} \times \dfrac{3}{4} =$ _______________

106. $\dfrac{5}{7} \times \dfrac{2}{3} =$ _______________

Mixed Numbers: Improper Fractions

1. $7\frac{9}{14} =$ _______________

2. $\frac{67}{30} =$ _______________

3. $\frac{94}{22} =$ _______________

4. $1\frac{3}{8} =$ _______________

5. $3\frac{1}{18} =$ _______________

6. $\frac{166}{26} =$ _______________

7. $\frac{39}{6} =$ _______________

8. $3\frac{4}{6} =$ _______________

9. $\frac{289}{34} =$ _______________

10. $6\frac{14}{19} =$ _______________

11. $3\frac{6}{8} =$ _______________

12. $\frac{82}{14} =$ _______________

Name:_______________________ Date: ____________

13. $\dfrac{27}{6}$ = _______________________

14. $5\dfrac{2}{16}$ = _______________________

15. $6\dfrac{2}{8}$ = _______________________

16. $6\dfrac{2}{4}$ = _______________________

17. $\dfrac{238}{36}$ = _______________________

18. $5\dfrac{5}{7}$ = _______________________

19. $\dfrac{21}{4}$ = _______________________

20. $\dfrac{118}{14}$ = _______________________

21. $6\dfrac{20}{24}$ = _______________________

22. $6\dfrac{11}{22}$ = _______________________

23. $4\dfrac{9}{16}$ = _______________________

24. $\dfrac{282}{40}$ = _______________________

25. $1\dfrac{15}{18}$ = _______________________

26. $\dfrac{162}{26}$ = _______________________

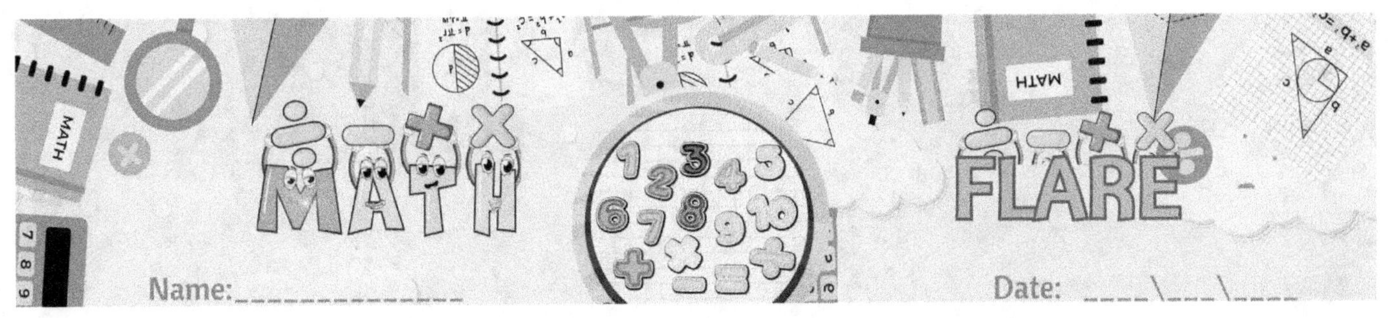

27. $3\frac{1}{30} =$ __________

28. $\frac{137}{28} =$ __________

29. $1\frac{1}{3} =$ __________

30. $\frac{233}{26} =$ __________

31. $8\frac{39}{40} =$ __________

32. $\frac{127}{16} =$ __________

33. $4\frac{4}{17} =$ __________

34. $8\frac{11}{12} =$ __________

35. $\frac{6}{4} =$ __________

36. $\frac{51}{20} =$ __________

37. $7\frac{1}{7} =$ __________

38. $2\frac{3}{8} =$ __________

39. $\frac{29}{14} =$ __________

40. $5\frac{15}{18} =$ __________

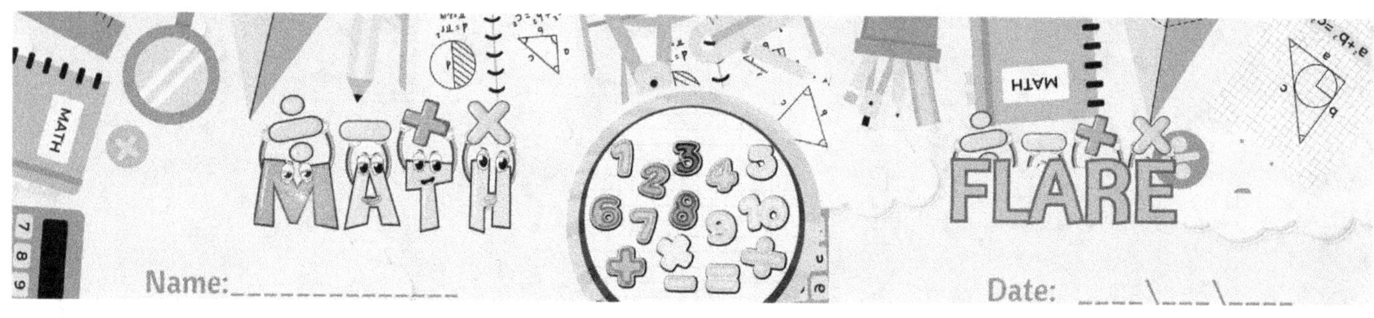

Fractions Addition Word Problems

1. Grace bought $\frac{1}{4}$ of a pound of cheese and then added another $\frac{1}{2}$ of a pound to make a sandwich. How much cheese did she use in total?

2. Hunter practiced math for $\frac{1}{6}$ of an hour and then played video games for another $\frac{2}{3}$ of an hour. How much time did he spend on these activities in total?

3. A recipe calls for $\frac{2}{7}$ cups of strawberries and $\frac{5}{10}$ cups of bananas. How much fruit is needed in total for the recipe?

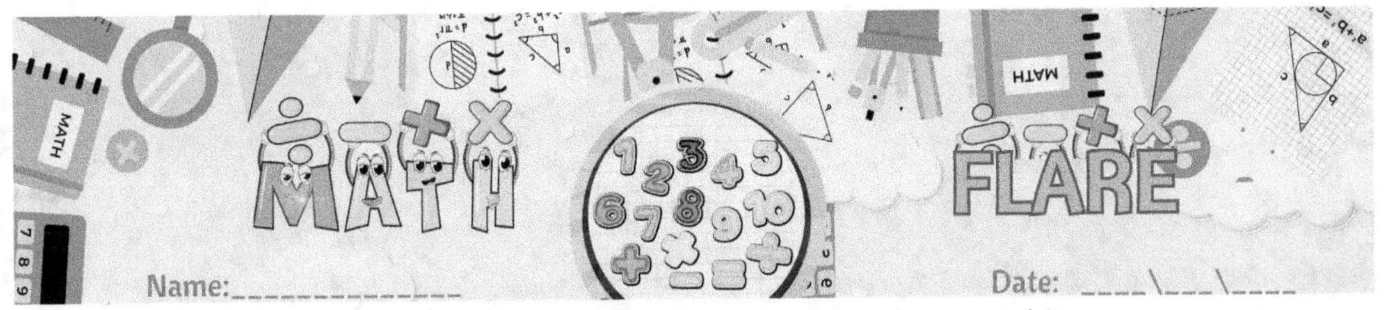

4. Zara made a salad with $\frac{1}{2}$ of a cup of lettuce and $\frac{1}{4}$ of a cup of spinach. How much salad did she make in total?

5. David spent $\frac{4}{7}$ of his allowance on a flosses and then spent another $\frac{2}{7}$ of his allowance on a video game. How much money did he spend in total?

6. Joshua paints $\frac{1}{3}$ of his paintnig on Monday, and $\frac{5}{8}$ on Tuesday. How much of his painting has he finished in total?

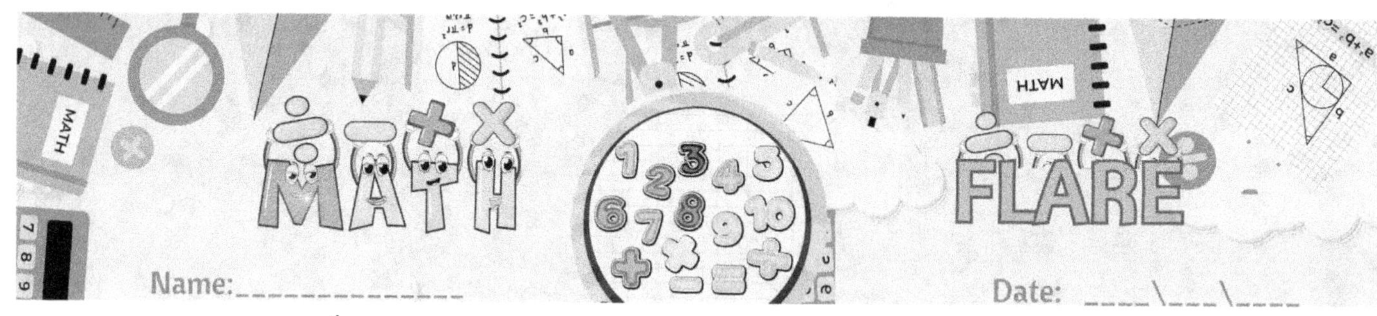

7. Alice used $\frac{1}{5}$ of a stick of butter in a recipe and then used another $\frac{1}{2}$ of the stick in a different recipe. How much of the stick did she use in total?

8. A car travels $\frac{1}{4}$ of a mile at a constant speed and then travels another $\frac{2}{4}$ of a mile at a different constant speed. How far did the car travel in total?

9. Alexander drank $\frac{1}{7}$ of a bottle of juice and then drank another $\frac{3}{9}$ of the bottle later. How much of the bottle did he drink in total?

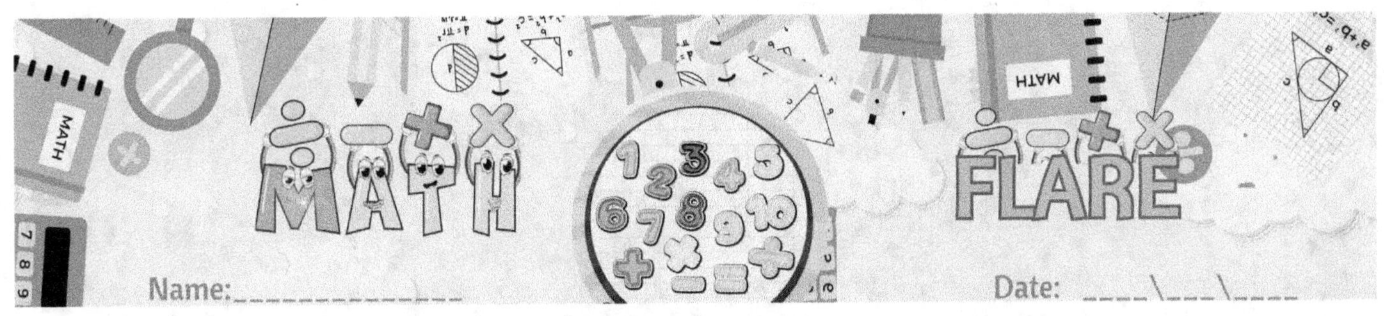

10. Oliver ate $\frac{3}{5}$ of a pizza for lunch and then ate another $\frac{3}{8}$ of the pizza for dinner. How much of the pizza did he eat in total?

11. Natalia spent $\frac{2}{3}$ of her salary on globes and then $\frac{1}{5}$ of the money on food. How much money did she spend?

12. Evelyn walked $\frac{1}{6}$ miles to the store and then walked back home another $\frac{3}{6}$ miles. How far did she walk in total?

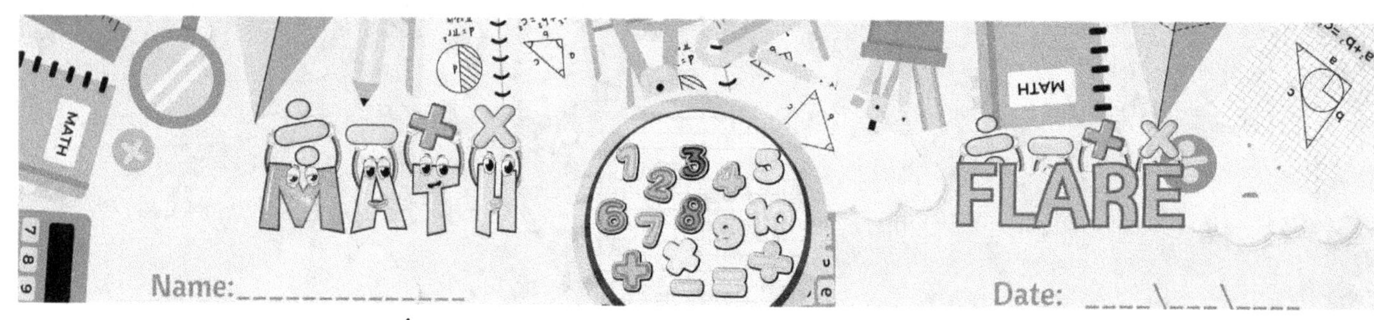

13. Aaron walked $\frac{1}{5}$ of a mile to the store and then walked another $\frac{2}{3}$ of a mile back home. How far did he walk in total?

14. If the sum of two fractions is $\frac{17}{24}$ and the first fraction is $\frac{1}{3}$, what is the second fraction?

15. Kingston writes $\frac{1}{2}$ of his paper before lunch. After lunch, he writes $\frac{1}{2}$ more. How much of his paper has he finished in total?

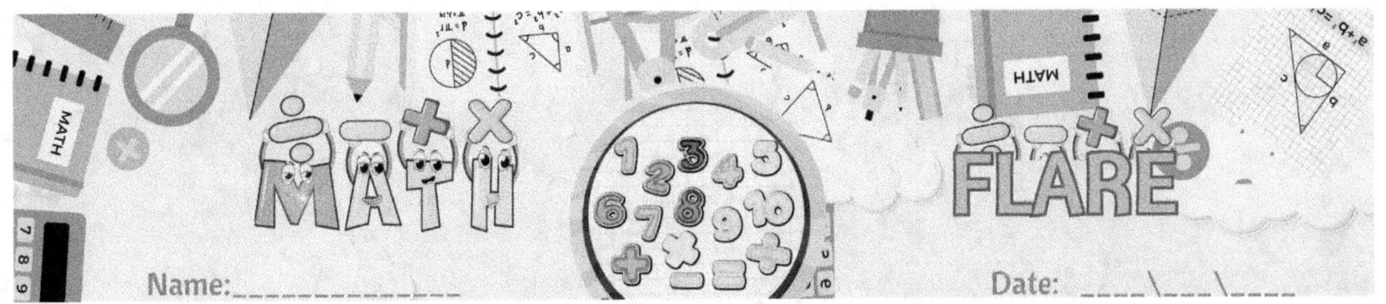

16. A recipe calls for $\frac{1}{7}$ cups of flour and $\frac{2}{6}$ cups of sugar. How much dry ingredient in total is needed for the recipe?

17. Emma finished $\frac{2}{4}$ of a book and then read $\frac{2}{8}$ of the remaining pages. How much of the book has she read?

18. A juice recipe calls for $\frac{2}{8}$ cups of orange juice and $\frac{2}{3}$ cups of apple juice. How much juice is needed in total for the recipe?

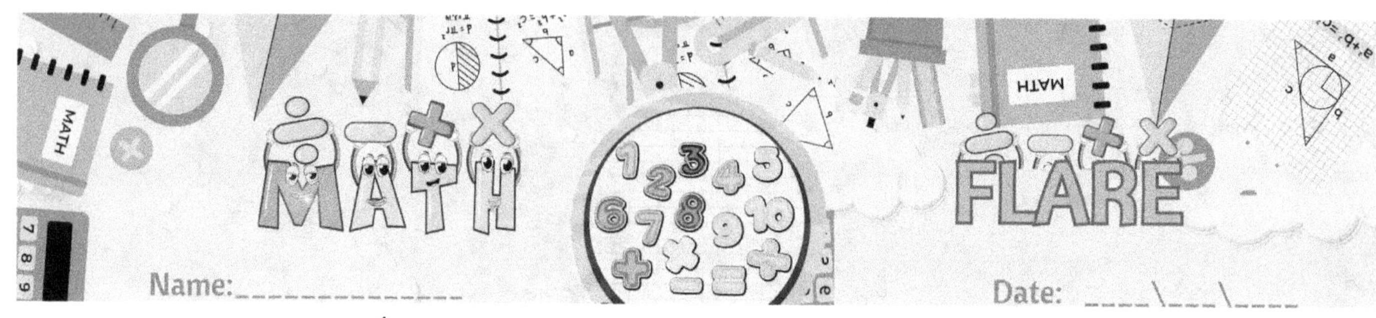

19. Stella cycled $\frac{1}{2}$ miles. She then stopped to buy some groceries. Then she cycled $\frac{3}{7}$ more miles. How far did Stella cycle in total?

20. Isaac drove $\frac{4}{7}$ of a mile and then walked $\frac{3}{10}$ of a mile to his friend's house. How far did he travel in total?

21. Aurora baked $\frac{2}{5}$ of her cakes for her friends and then kept $\frac{1}{2}$ of them for herself. How many cakes did she bake in total?

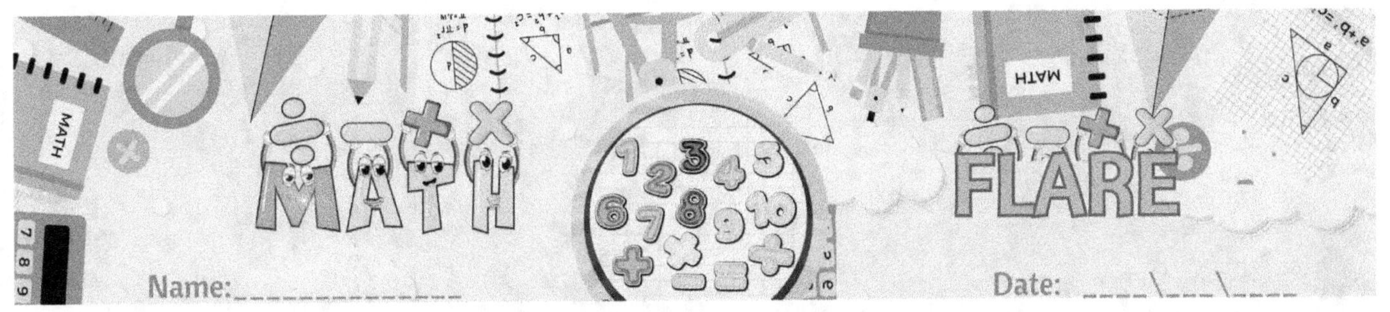

Fractions Subtraction Word Problems

1. A recipe calls for $\frac{9}{10}$ of a cup of sugar. If $\frac{1}{4}$ of the sugar is already used, how much sugar is left in cups?

2. Leah is making a sweet dish and needs $\frac{5}{8}$ of a cup of strawberries. She has already used $\frac{1}{3}$ of a cup. How much more strawberry does she need?

3. Adalyn has $\frac{4}{9}$ of a container of shirts. She gives $\frac{1}{4}$ of the shirts to her sister. How much shirts does she have left?

4. Caroline needs $\frac{6}{7}$ of a cup of sugar to make lemonade. She only has $\frac{3}{8}$ of a cup of sugar. How much more sugar does she need to make the lemonade?

5. James and Luna are cooking dinner and need $\frac{5}{6}$ of a cup of oil. James accidentally spills $\frac{4}{8}$ of a cup of oil. How much oil do they have left?

6. Wyatt has a rope that is $\frac{5}{7}$ of a meter long. If he cuts off $\frac{1}{3}$ of the rope, how long is the remaining rope in meters?

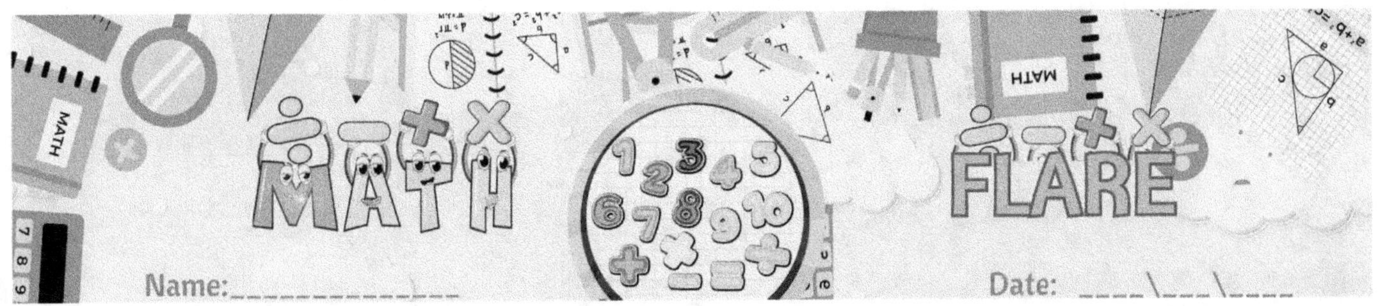

7. Samuel has $\frac{8}{10}$ of a pound of cheese. He uses $\frac{3}{4}$ of the cheese to make a sandwich. How much cheese is left in pounds?

8. Elizabeth has $\frac{6}{7}$ of a pound of ground chicken. She uses $\frac{2}{5}$ of the chicken to make a burger. How much chicken is left in pounds?

9. Isabelle needs $\frac{4}{10}$ of a pound of cheese to make pizza. She only has $\frac{2}{7}$ of a pound of cheese. How much more cheese does she need to buy?

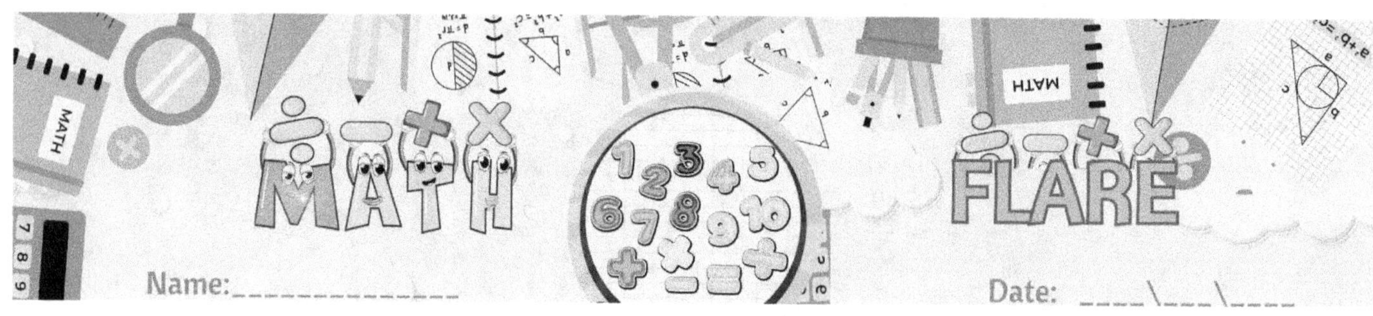

10. Dylan has a length of ribbon that is $\frac{1}{2}$ meters long. He wants to cut off $\frac{3}{8}$ of the ribbon to use for a gift. How long will the remaining ribbon be?

11. Jace has a collection of microphones that weighs $\frac{4}{6}$ of a pound. If he loses $\frac{1}{2}$ of the weight, how much does the collection now weigh in pounds?

12. Emma has a book that is $\frac{1}{6}$ of an inch thick. She reads $\frac{1}{8}$ of the book. How thick is the remaining portion of the book in inches?

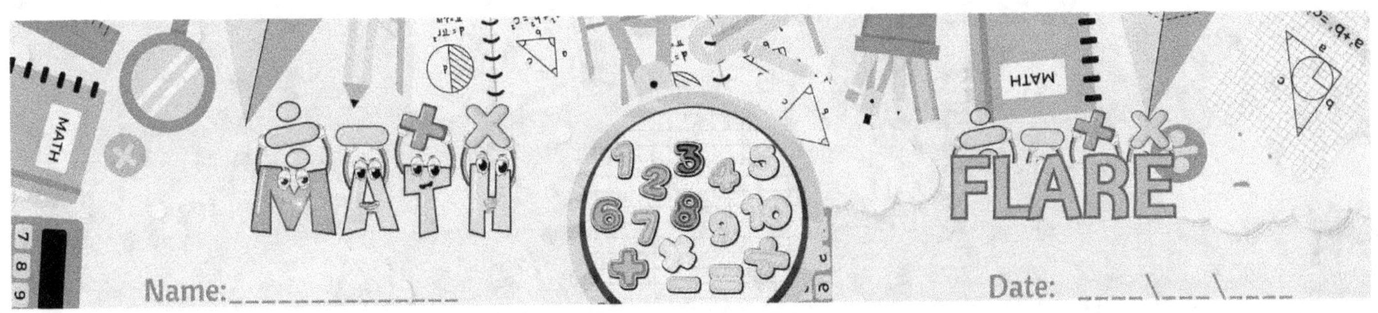

13. Evelyn is running on a track that is $\frac{7}{9}$ of a mile long. She has already run $\frac{4}{9}$ of the mile. How much further does she have to run?

14. Elena wants to make a dish that calls for $\frac{6}{7}$ of a cup of yogurt. She only has $\frac{1}{2}$ of a cup of yogurt left. How much more yogurt does she need to make the dish?

15. Justin filled his water bottle with $\frac{2}{4}$ of a liter of water before going for a walk. During the walk, he drank $\frac{3}{7}$ of the water. How much water does he have left in the bottle?

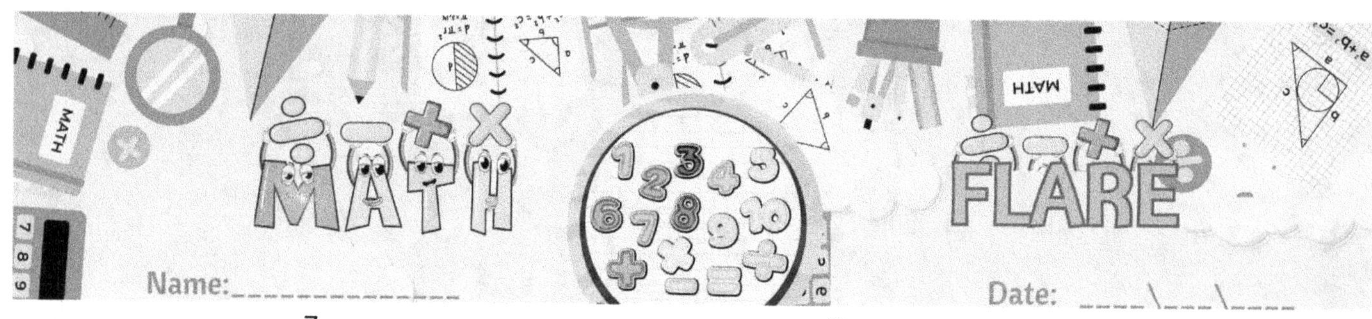

16. Jose has $\frac{7}{9}$ of a liter of juice. He drinks $\frac{3}{8}$ of the juice. How much juice is left in liters?

17. Jordyn has $\frac{2}{5}$ of a pound of flour. She uses $\frac{2}{9}$ of the flour to make a pencake. How much flour is left in pounds?

18. Audrey bought a bag of flour that weighed $\frac{7}{9}$ pounds. She used $\frac{1}{6}$ of the flour to make pencakes. How much flour was left in the bag?

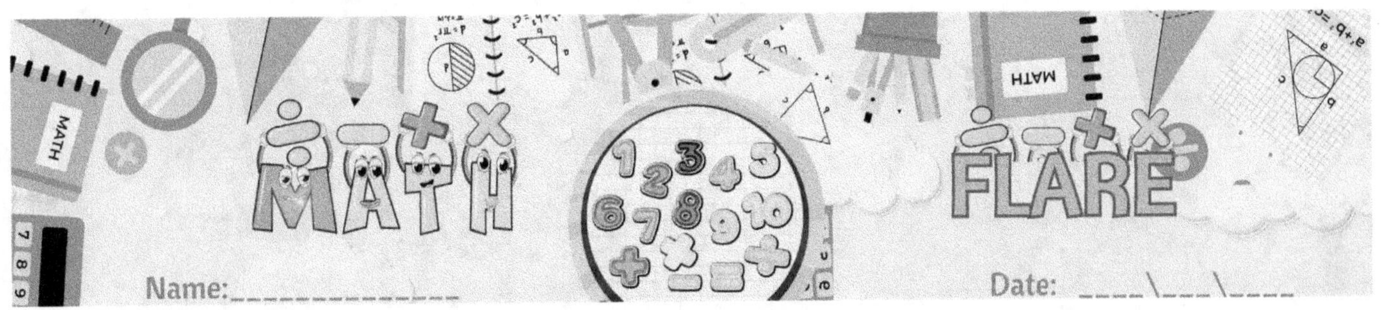

19. Alice has $\frac{7}{9}$ of a pound of beef. She cooks $\frac{1}{3}$ of the beef. How much beef is left in pounds?

20. Abigail is painting a room with a can of paint that has $\frac{5}{8}$ gallons in it. She has used $\frac{2}{4}$ of the paint so far. How much paint is left in the can?

21. Lucas has $\frac{1}{3}$ of a liter of water. He drinks $\frac{1}{9}$ of the water. How much water is left in liters?

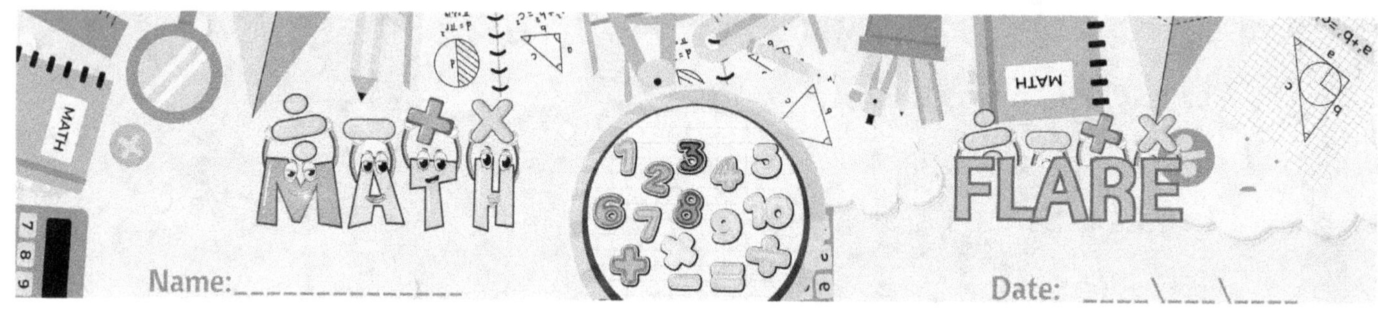

Fractions Multiplication Word Problems

1. A bike tire has a radius of $\frac{2}{4}$ foot. If the tire rolls 6 times, how far does the bike travel?

2. Cooper needs $\frac{6}{10}$ cup of flour for a recipe and he wants to make $\frac{3}{4}$ batches of the recipe, how much flour will he need in total?

3. If a recipe calls for $\frac{2}{7}$ cup of butter and you want to make $\frac{6}{9}$ as much, how much butter do you need?

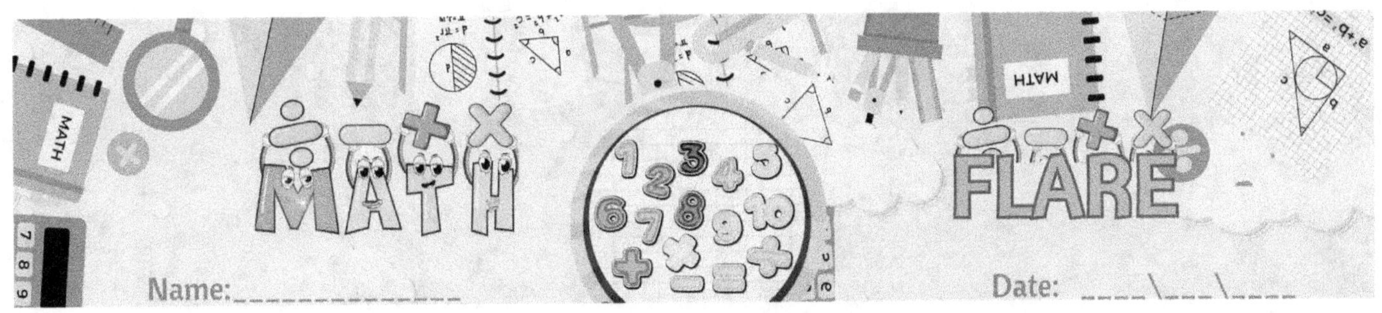

4. If a recipe calls for $\frac{6}{10}$ cup of flour and you want to make it 5, how much flour do you need?

5. If a company can produce $\frac{3}{4}$ of a product in one day, how many days will it take to produce 4 products?

6. A factory can produce $\frac{2}{4}$ of a car in one hour. How many cars can the factory produce in 8 hours?

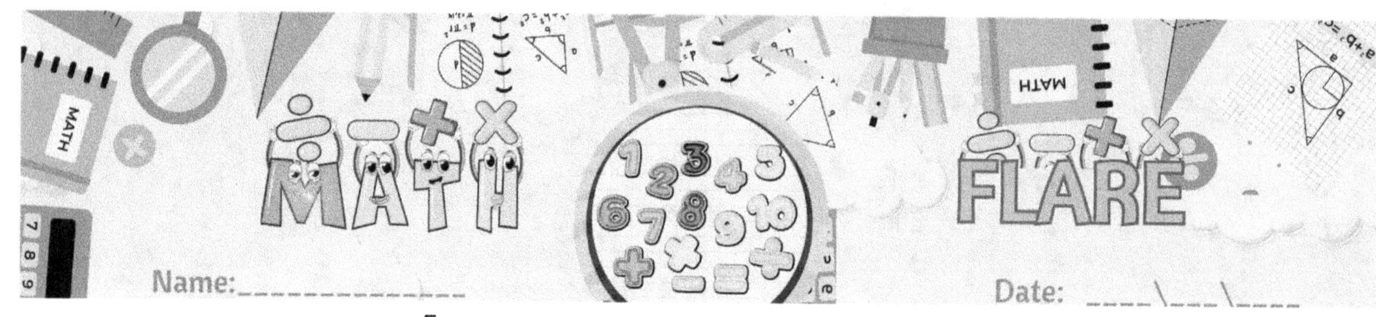

7. William walked $\frac{5}{8}$ of a mile every day for 7 days. How many miles did he walk in total?

8. If you need to make 5 batches of cookies, and each batch requires $\frac{2}{5}$ cup of chocolate chips, how many cups of chocolate chips do you need in total?

9. If a container holds $\frac{2}{10}$ of a gallon of water and you need 3 gallons of water, how many containers do you need?

10. Grace ran $\frac{3}{5}$ miles every day for 10 days. How many miles did she run in total?

11. If a car can travel $\frac{1}{2}$ of a mile on one gallon of gas, how many miles can it travel on 3 gallons of gas?

12. If a bag of flour weighs $\frac{2}{9}$ of a pound and you need $\frac{7}{10}$ bags, how many pounds of flour do you need in total?

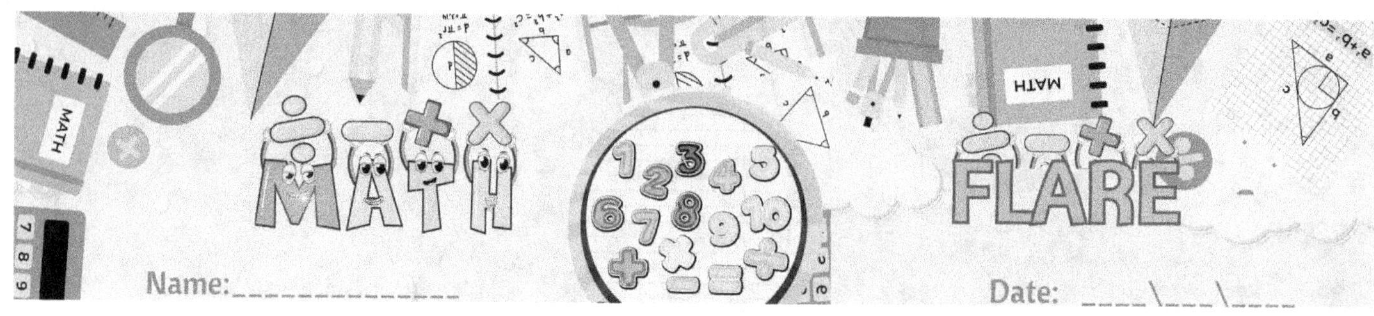

13. A school needs to make 100 cupcakes for a fundraiser. If a batch of cupcakes requires $\frac{1}{3}$ cups of sugar, how many cups of sugar will they need in total?

14. Sebastian is making a dish that calls for $\frac{8}{10}$ cup of cooking oil. If he wants to make 2 dishes of the same recipe, how much cooking oil does he need?

15. If a garden has an area of $\frac{4}{8}$ square feet and you want to increase it by a factor of 2, what will be the new area of the garden?

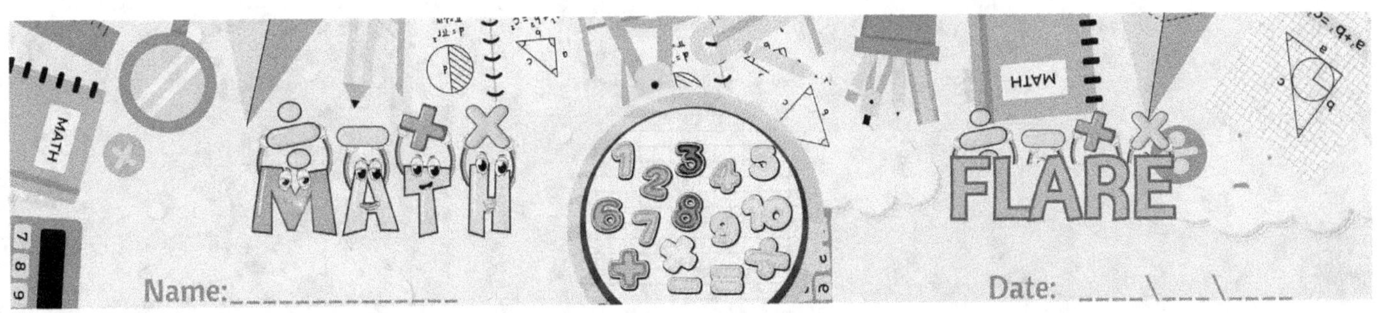

16. If a person can run at a speed of $\frac{5}{6}$ miles per hour, how long will it take him to run 4 miles?

17. A cake recipe calls for $\frac{5}{7}$ cups of sugar to make one cake. If Zara wants to make 6 cakes, how many cups of sugar will she need?

18. Olivia drove $\frac{4}{5}$ of the distance to the mall. If the distance to the mall is $\frac{6}{10}$ miles, how far did Olivia drive?

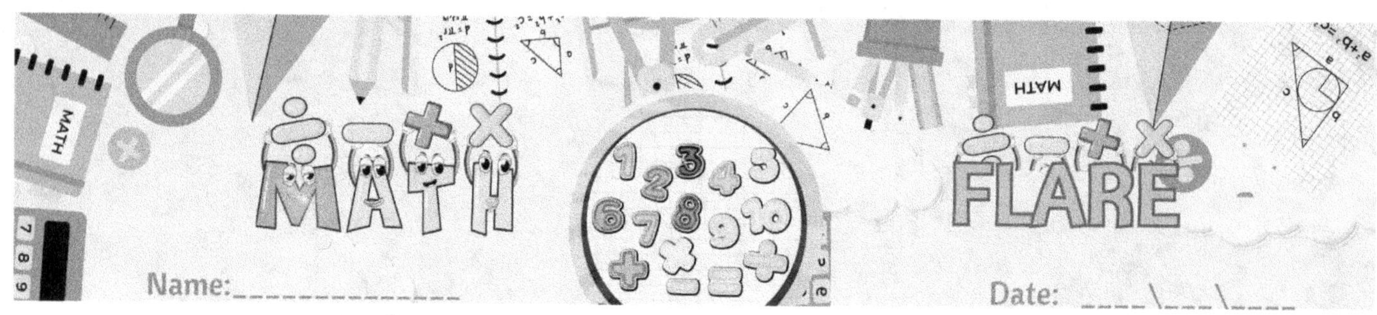

19. Emma needs $\frac{6}{10}$ cup of milk to make 1 cup of coffee, how much milk is needed to make 4 cups of coffee?

20. If a recipe calls for $\frac{2}{4}$ cup of milk and you want to make $\frac{6}{10}$ times as much, how much milk do you need?

21. Adam spent $\frac{2}{5}$ of his money to buy deodorants. His friend David spent 3 times more to buy the deodorants. How much did David spend?

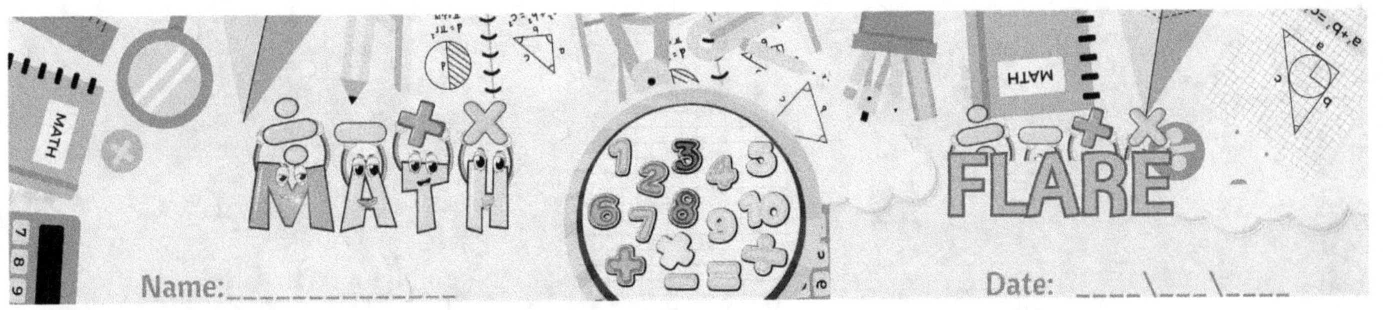

Fractions Division Word Problems

1. If you have $\frac{1}{2}$ of a cake and you want to divide it equally among 5 people, what fraction of the cake will each person get?

2. If you have $\frac{1}{6}$ of a gallon of water and you want to divide it equally among 2 jugs, what fraction of a gallon of water will each jug get?

3. If you have $\frac{4}{7}$ of a pizza and you want to share it equally with 4 friends, what fraction of the pizza will each friend get?

4. Miles has $\frac{3}{9}$ of a cup of juice and he wants to divide it equally into 5 cups, what fraction of a cup of juice will each cup get?

5. If you have $\frac{3}{8}$ of a pie and you want to share it equally with 3 friends, what fraction of the pie will each friend get?

6. If you have $\frac{6}{7}$ of a pound of cheese and you want to divide it equally among 4 sandwiches, what fraction of a pound of cheese will each sandwich get?

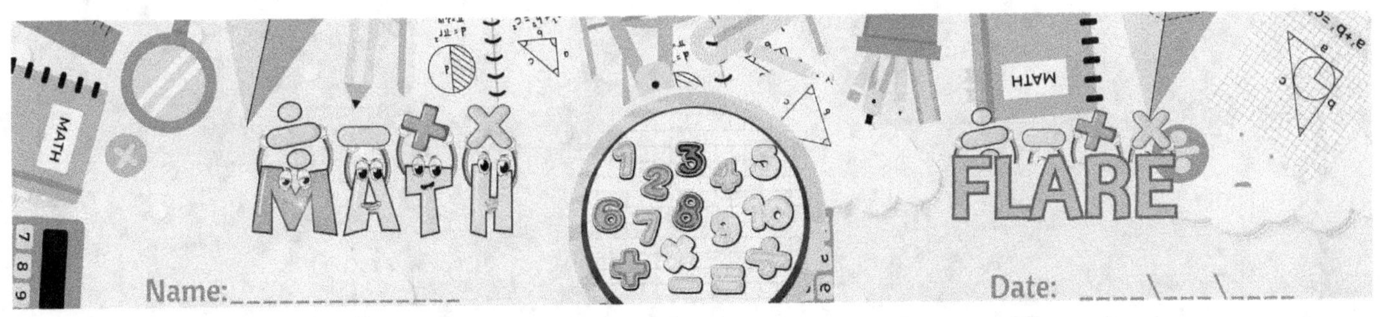

7. If you have $\frac{5}{10}$ of a cup of sugar and you want to divide it equally into 2 bowls, what fraction of a cup of sugar will each bowl get?

8. If you divide $\frac{2}{3}$ by $\frac{2}{3}$, what is the answer?

9. If a bottle contains $\frac{4}{5}$ of a liter of juice and you want to split it equally between 3 people, how much juice will each person get?

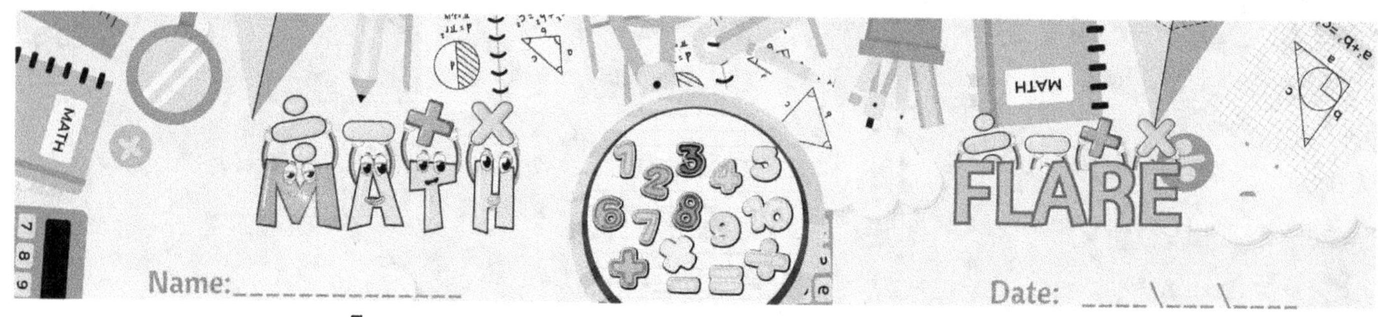

10. If you have $\frac{5}{6}$ of a pound of ground beef and you want to make 6 patties, how much beef is needed for each patty?

11. Hannah has $\frac{2}{4}$ of a pound of beef and she wants to divide it equally among 3 burgers, what fraction of a pound of beef will each burger get?

12. If a farmer has $\frac{1}{2}$ of an acre of land to plant corn, and he wants to divide the land equally into 3 parts, how much land will each part have?

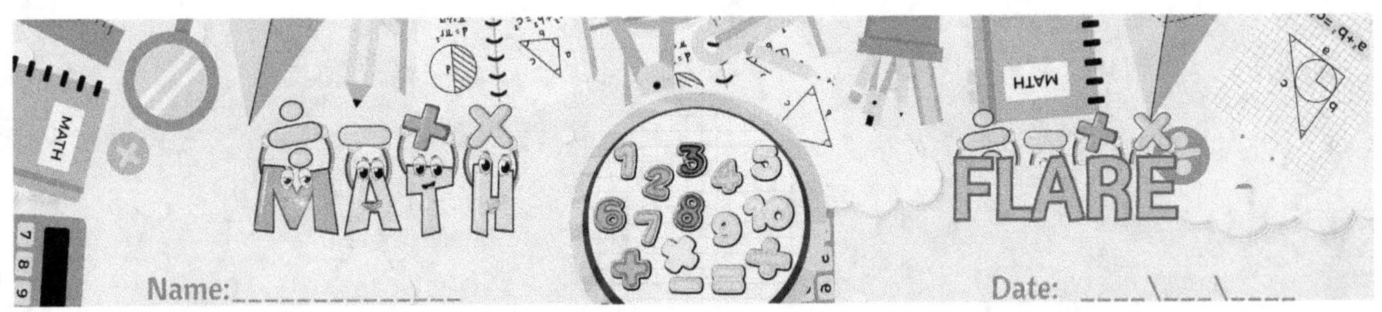

13. Ellie has $\frac{7}{9}$ of a bag of gloves and she wants to divide it equally among 3 people, what fraction of the bag of gloves will each person get?

14. Lila has $\frac{2}{7}$ of a pound of beef and she wants to divide it equally among 3 burgers, what fraction of a pound of beef will each burger get?

15. If you divide $\frac{4}{9}$ by $\frac{7}{9}$, what is the answer?

16. If a farmer has $\frac{1}{3}$ of an acre of land to plant corn, and he wants to divide the land equally into 3 parts, how much land will each part have?

17. If you have $\frac{2}{6}$ of a pound of ground beef and you want to make 6 patties, how much beef is needed for each patty?

18. If you have $\frac{4}{8}$ of a cup of sugar and you want to divide it equally into 2 bowls, what fraction of a cup of sugar will each bowl get?

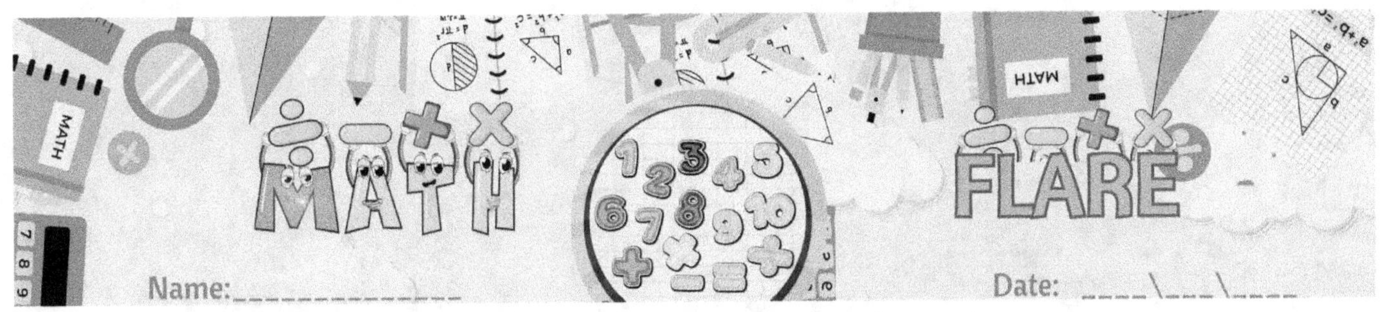

19. If you have $\frac{1}{4}$ of a pound of cheese and you want to divide it equally among 4 sandwiches, what fraction of a pound of cheese will each sandwich get?

20. If you have $\frac{2}{10}$ of a cake and you want to divide it equally among 5 people, what fraction of the cake will each person get?

21. If you have $\frac{1}{2}$ of a pizza and you want to share it equally with 4 friends, what fraction of the pizza will each friend get?

ANSWERS

Page 1:   Equivalent Fractions

1. 56, 21	2. 63, 72	3. 50, 15	4. 21, 27	5. 36, 35
6. 30, 68	7. 48, 24	8. 3, 2	9. 160, 120	10. 54, 120
11. 60, 75	12. 26, 44	13. 120, 42	14. 81, 90	15. 32, 24
16. 36, 18	17. 32, 80	18. 4, 6	19. 30, 12	20. 128, 64
21. 33, 28	22. 45, 30	23. 56, 21	24. 72, 14	25. 28, 70
26. 128, 160	27. 39, 8	28. 30, 60	29. 24, 15	30. 30, 135
31. 45, 8	32. 3, 16	33. 36, 24	34. 54, 80	35. 12, 16
36. 18, 40	37. 18, 60	38. 36, 35	39. 30, 8	40. 160, 72
41. 7, 9	42. 16, 14	43. 190, 57	44. 135, 35	45. 30, 20
46. 30, 48	47. 68, 105	48. 36, 8	49. 24, 10	50. 90, 54
51. 64, 120	52. 110, 8	53. 63, 12	54. 54, 42	55. 3, 4
56. 14, 4	57. 45, 14	58. 10, 100		

Page 6:   Fractions Addition: Uncommon Denominator

1. 29/40	2. 4/5	3. 71/112	4. 23/30	5. 11/20
6. 41/57	7. 86/105	8. 7/12	9. 5/7	10. 67/90
11. 31/55	12. 5/8	13. 11/18	14. 17/20	15. 92/117
16. 29/66	17. 9/14	18. 67/140	19. 64/85	20. 67/90
21. 13/18	22. 159/304	23. 5/9	24. 19/30	25. 151/340
26. 5/7	27. 97/152	28. 173/176	29. 17/20	30. 26/55

31. 5/8   32. 52/55   33. 61/80   34. 91/152   35. 35/39

36. 117/170   37. 35/66   38. 13/36   39. 19/30   40. 169/228

41. 1/2   42. 70/143   43. 11/28   44. 11/12   45. 17/18

46. 11/14   47. 37/51   48. 29/52   49. 7/8   50. 13/16

51. 23/30   52. 4/5   53. 9/14   54. 2/3   55. 27/28

56. 67/95   57. 37/40   58. 32/33   59. 19/20   60. 111/119

61. 4/9   62. 167/176   63. 20/21   64. 203/285   65. 39/40

66. 117/119   67. 3/5   68. 6/7   69. 57/70   70. 3/4

71. 19/24   72. 13/22   73. 14/15   74. 59/88   75. 57/170

76. 13/21   77. 33/34   78. 41/126   79. 13/15   80. 130/171

81. 127/170   82. 4/9   83. 19/35   84. 20/21   85. 4/7

86. 8/11   87. 2/3   88. 61/76   89. 79/80   90. 3/10

91. 49/60   92. 83/132   93. 3/4   94. 272/285   95. 5/6

96. 45/208

Page 13: Fractions Subtraction - Uncommon Denominator

1. 46/105   2. 13/40   3. 1/4   4. 1/35   5. 4/9

6. 1/76   7. 167/234   8. 1/4   9. 13/63   10. 13/51

11. 3/44   12. 124/171   13. 13/84   14. 5/12   15. 50/117

16. 9/170   17. 5/21   18. 233/266   19. 19/33   20. 23/35

21. 3/20   22. 2/5   23. 4/13   24. 7/68   25. 2/7

26. 19/132   27. 2/5   28. 4/15   29. 3/14   30. 5/22

31. 22/91   32. 2/15   33. 2/9   34. 1/42   35. 7/18

36. 1/38   37. 121/266   38. 9/35   39. 3/20   40. 1/30

41. 27/52   42. 23/144   43. 79/180   44. 24/55   45. 1/3

46. 1/10   47. 13/36   48. 35/156   49. 13/88   50. 47/126

51. 127/153   52. 4/187   53. 1/4   54. 29/60   55. 5/12

56. 11/38   57. 1/4   58. 1/4   59. 85/152   60. 19/55

61. 9/52   62. 1/20   63. 31/51   64. 1/6   65. 26/57

66. 11/40   67. 19/33   68. 11/24   69. 19/52   70. 211/342

71. 3/16   72. 29/57   73. 6/17   74. 13/28   75. 5/18

76. 1/12   77. 11/80   78. 1/2   79. 17/78   80. 27/40

81. 9/68   82. 3/26   83. 3/10   84. 3/28   85. 3/11

86. 8/57   87. 61/102   88. 5/12   89. 61/255   90. 13/102

91. 129/266   92. 3/40   93. 7/16   94. 1/10

Page 21: Fractions Multiplication

1. 1/18   2. 7/10   3. 5/12   4. 11/35   5. 4/9

6. 4/11   7. 12/91   8. 7/15   9. 9/32   10. 9/35

11. 4/15   12. 22/65   13. 15/22   14. 13/18   15. 9/160

16. 1/45   17. 1/12   18. 1/3   19. 1/7   20. 2/9

21. 3/25   22. 3/14   23. 36/143   24. 3/80   25. 5/24

26. 2/33   27. 5/48   28. 1/6   29. 5/48   30. 91/160

31. 4/27   32. 56/165   33. 5/14   34. 8/45   35. 3/14

36. 4/9	37. 3/8	38. 1/12	39. 1/78	40. 35/208
41. 1/7	42. 3/5	43. 45/56	44. 13/30	45. 3/20
46. 18/91	47. 3/11	48. 4/15	49. 1/28	50. 8/15
51. 3/28	52. 1/52	53. 5/24	54. 18/55	55. 1/4
56. 22/75	57. 9/14	58. 27/80	59. 49/99	60. 2/7
61. 1/8	62. 3/40	63. 1/15	64. 3/25	65. 3/13
66. 3/22	67. 5/49	68. 3/56	69. 1/9	70. 14/25
71. 3/8	72. 2/11	73. 1/10	74. 1/13	75. 1/7
76. 1/10	77. 11/15	78. 13/24	79. 1/16	80. 2/5
81. 10/27	82. 2/49	83. 1/24	84. 7/120	85. 9/224
86. 36/77	87. 3/10	88. 1/5	89. 5/14	90. 49/240
91. 2/9	92. 7/24	93. 2/21	94. 4/45	95. 12/169
96. 1/6	97. 5/24	98. 10/77	99. 1/2	100. 12/65
101. 15/32	102. 28/135	103. 4/21	104. 1/3	105. 3/8
106. 10/21				

Page 30: Mixed Numbers: Improper Fractions

1. 107/14	2. 2 7/30	3. 4 3/11	4. 11/8	5. 55/18
6. 6 5/13	7. 6 1/2	8. 11/3	9. 8 1/2	10. 128/19
11. 15/4	12. 5 6/7	13. 4 1/2	14. 41/8	15. 25/4
16. 13/2	17. 6 11/18	18. 40/7	19. 5 1/4	20. 8 3/7
21. 41/6	22. 13/2	23. 73/16	24. 7 1/20	25. 11/6

26. 6 3/13   27. 91/30   28. 4 25/28   29. 4/3   30. 8 25/26

31. 359/40   32. 7 15/16   33. 72/17   34. 107/12   35. 1 1/2

36. 2 11/20   37. 50/7   38. 19/8   39. 2 1/14   40. 35/6

Page 33:   Fractions Addition Word Problems

1. 3/4   2. 5/6   3. 11/14   4. 3/4   5. 6/7   6. 23/24

7. 7/10   8. 3/4   9. 10/21   10. 39/40   11. 13/15   12. 2/3

13. 13/15   14. 3/8   15. 1   16. 10/21   17. 3/4   18. 11/12

19. 13/14   20. 61/70   21. 9/10

Page 40:   Fractions Subtraction Word Problems

1. 13/20   2. 7/24   3. 7/36   4. 27/56   5. 1/3   6. 8/21

7. 1/20   8. 16/35   9. 4/35   10. 1/8   11. 1/6   12. 1/24

13. 1/3   14. 5/14   15. 1/14   16. 29/72   17. 8/45   18. 11/18

19. 4/9   20. 1/8   21. 2/9

Page 47:   Fractions Multiplication Word Problems

1. 3   2. 9/20   3. 4/21   4. 3   5. 3   6. 4

7. 35/8   8. 2   9. 3/5   10. 6   11. 3/2   12. 7/45

13. 100/3   14. 8/5   15. 1   16. 10/3   17. 30/7   18. 12/25

19. 12/5   20. 3/10   21. 6/5

Page 54:   Fractions Division Word Problems

1. 1/10   2. 1/12   3. 1/7   4. 1/15   5. 1/8   6. 3/14   7. 1/4

8. 1   9. 4/15   10. 5/36   11. 1/6   12. 1/6   13. 7/27   14. 2/21

15. 4/7   16. 1/9   17. 1/18   18. 1/4   19. 1/16   20. 1/25   21. 1/8